문법이 저절로

3 STEP

Writing

2

I am books

Preview

1
Writing에 필요한 문법
해당 Unit의 영작을 위해 필요한 문법사항을
학습합니다.

2
Writing에 필요한 문법 확인
문제풀이를 통해 앞에서 배운 문법사항을
확인합니다.

3
Warm Up: 표현 만들기
해당 Unit의 영작을 위해 필요한 기본
표현을 익히고 써봅니다.

4
Step 1: 문장 만들기
Warm Up에서 학습한 표현을 활용하여
기본 문장들을 영작합니다.

5

Step 2: 문장 완성하기

수식어 또는 수식어구를 활용하여 Step 1에서
만든 기본 문장들을 완성합니다.

6

Step 3: 문장 꾸미기

수식어 또는 수식어구를 활용하여 Step 2에서 완
성한 문장들을 더욱 확장된 장문으로 써봅니다.

7

More Practice

영작 문제를 통해 학습한 내용을 복습합니다.

8

Creative Thinking Activity

다양한 유형의 활동을 통해 학습한 영작 Skill을
적용 및 응용합니다.

영작을 위한 학생들의 이해도를
돕기 위해 간혹 어색한
한국말 표현이 있을 수 있음을
알려드립니다.

Contents

등위접속사

 Writing에 필요한 문법

1. 등위접속사란?

- 단어와 단어, 구와 구, 또는 문장과 문장을 대등하게 연결하는 단어
- and, but, or

2. 등위접속사가 있는 문장 맛보기

3. 등위접속사의 쓰임

종류	쓰임	예문	해석
and	① 서로 비슷한 내용을 연결 ② 셋 이상의 단어를 나열할 때에는 마지막 단어 앞에 comma(,)와 and를 쓴다. (comma 생략 가능)	Jane and Sally are good friends. Tony likes apples, bananas(,) and peaches. Tom plays the piano and I play the violin at the concert.	-와, 그리고
but	서로 반대되는 내용을 연결	The bear looks scary but cute. I am tall but my sister is short.	그러나
or	① 선택할 내용을 연결 ② 셋 이상의 단어를 나열할 때에는 마지막 단어 앞에 comma(,)와 or을 쓴다. (comma 생략 가능)	Do you want some milk or juice? I will go to France, Italy(,) or England this summer. Let's meet on Saturday or Sunday.	또는

📣 Writing에 필요한 문법 확인

A. 알맞은 등위접속사를 넣어 문장을 완성하시오.

1 Do you want to go swimming _____ go hiking?

2 She bought a skirt _____ a jacket.

3 I like English _____ I don't like math.

4 Bill went to school _____ he studied hard.

5 Amy was sad _____ she didn't cry.

B. comma(,)가 필요한 곳에 체크(v)하시오. comma(,)가 필요 없다면 X표 하시오.

1 David got a toy car a book and a ball for his birthday.

2 I read two or three books every month.

3 Which color do you like, yellow, green or blue?

4 The baker needs some sugar salt, and flour to make cookies.

5 He was poor but happy.

C. 주어진 단어를 사용하여 문장을 완성하시오.

1 Kevin / his mom / loves / dad / and / .

_____

2 the problem looks / is simple / difficult / but / .

_____

3 some bread / you / like / would / or rice / ?

_____

4 need a pencil / I / a note book / and an eraser / , / , / .

_____

5 or a hat / I will / a bag / buy a scarf / , / , / .

_____

English	Korean	English	Korean
Chinese	n. 중국어	shoes	n. 신발
class	n. 수업	singer	n. 가수
expensive	adj. 값이 비싼	Spanish	n. 스페인어
fast	adj. 빠른	steak	n. 스테이크
fishing	n. 낚시	swimming	n. 수영
leave	v. 떠나다	vegetable	n. 채소
pasta	n. 파스타	work out	운동하다

다음의 우리말 표현을 영어로 쓰시오.

1 사과와 샌드위치

    an apple and a sandwich

2 스페인어 수업과 중국어 수업

3 채소들, 과일들, 그리고 꽃들

4 파스타, 밥, 또는 스테이크

5 수영과 낚시

6 아침과 저녁에

7 이번 주나 다음 주에

8 좋지만(nice) 비싼

9 오래됐지만 빠른

10 미소 짓지만(smile) 행복하지 않은

🐚 **다음의 우리말 표현을 영어로 쓰시오.**

1   나는   사과를   먹는다.

    I   eat   an apple.

    주어   동사   목적어

2   너는   스페인어 수업을   들었니 (take)?

_____

3   너는   채소들을   키우니 (grow)?

_____

4   나는   파스타를   요리할 것이다 (cook).

_____

5   그들은   수영을   즐겼다 (enjoy).

_____

6   그는   아침에   운동한다 .

_____

7   그녀는   이번 주에   떠날 것이다 .

_____

8   그 신발은   좋다 .

_____

9   나의 컴퓨터는   오래됐다 .

_____

10   그 가수는   미소 짓는다 .

_____

🐚 **다음의 우리말 표현을 영어로 쓰시오.**

1 나는 사과와 샌드위치를 먹는다.

   I eat an apple and a sandwich .

   _____

2 너는 스페인어 수업과 중국어 수업을 들었니?

   _____

3 너는 채소들, 과일들, 그리고 꽃들을 키우니?

   _____

4 나는 파스타, 밥, 또는 스테이크를 요리할 것이다.

   _____

5 그들은 수영과 낚시를 즐겼다.

   _____

6 그는 아침과 저녁에 운동한다.

   _____

7 그녀는 이번 주나 다음 주에 떠날 것이다.

   _____

8 그 신발은 좋지만 비싸다 .

   _____

9 나의 컴퓨터는 오래됐지만 빠르다 .

   _____

10 그 가수는 미소짓지만 그는 행복하지 않다 .

   _____

🐚 **다음의 우리말 표현을 영어로 쓰시오.**

1 나는 사과와 샌드위치를 **아침으로** 먹는다.

   I eat an apple and a sandwich **for breakfast** .

   _____

2 너는 **작년에** (last year) 스페인어 수업과 중국어 수업을 들었니?

   _____

3 너는 **정원에서** (in the garden) 채소들, 과일들, 그리고 꽃들을 키우니?

   _____

4 나는 **나의 친구들을 위해서** (for my friends) 파스타, 밥, 또는 스테이크를 요리할 것이다.

   _____

5 그들은 **바다에서** (in the sea) 수영과 낚시를 즐겼다.

   _____

6 그는 **건강을 위해** (for his health) 아침과 저녁에 운동한다.

   _____

7 그녀는 이번 주나 다음 주에 **캐나다로** (for Canada) 떠날 것이다.

   _____

8 **상점에 있는** (in the store) 그 신발은 좋지만 비싸다.

   _____

9 **책상 위에 있는** (on the desk) 나의 컴퓨터는 오래됐지만 빠르다.

   _____

10 **무대 위에 있는** (on stage) 그 가수는 미소 짓지만 그는 행복하지 않다.

   _____

Unit 2 상관접속사

 Writing에 필요한 문법

1. 상관접속사란?

- and, but, or, nor과 같은 등위 접속사가 다른 어구와 짝을 이루는 접속사
- 단어와 단어, 구와 구, 문장과 문장을 연결
- 강조의 의미가 있음

2. 상관접속사가 있는 문장 맛보기

STEP 1

| Sarah는 | 영어를 | 말한다 |.

| Sarah | speaks | English |.
주어　　　동사　　　목적어

STEP 2

Sarah는 | 영어와 스페인어 둘 다를 | 말한다.

Sarah speaks | both English and Spanish |.
both A and B: 상관접속사

STEP 3

Sarah는 | 국제 회의에서 | 영어와 스페인어 둘 다를 말한다.

Sarah speaks both English and Spanish | at the international meeting |.
수식어구

3. 상관접속사의 쓰임

종류	예문	해석
both A and B	Both David and Jason sing well.	A와 B 둘 다
not only A but also B = B as well as A	Sarah is not only smart but also beautiful. = Sarah is beautiful as well as smart.	A 뿐만 아니라 B도
not A but B	Tom is not a teacher but a student.	A가 아니라 B
either A or B	You can choose either pizza or spaghetti.	A와 B 둘 중 하나
neither A nor B	Neither I nor Jake has money.	A와 B 둘 다 아닌

* 위의 상관접속사들이 주어 자리에 올 경우, 동사는 B에 맞춘다. 단, both A and B는 복수 동사를 사용한다.
  Not only the children but also their uncle looks happy.　Both Jay and Sean live in Korea.

Writing에 필요한 문법 확인

A. 다음 중 알맞은 것을 고르시오.

1 Neither Tanya's dad (or / nor) mom speaks English.

2 David is not a baseball player (and / but) a basketball player.

3 Jake has both a brother (also / and) a sister.

4 This bird lives either in Korea (or / nor) in Japan.

5 Not only Jason (nor / but also) Sally skis well.

B. 주어진 두 문장이 같은 의미가 되도록 빈칸을 채우시오.

1 Sarah is good at not only writing but also reading.

= Sarah is good at _____ as well as _____.

2 David is not only a novelist but also a poet.

= David is _____ as well as _____.

3 Jason told Sarah not only his address but also his phone number.

= Jason told Sarah _____ as well as _____.

C. 상관접속사를 사용하여 문장을 완성하시오.

1 _____ Justin _____ Brian ate meat and fish.

(Justin과 Brian 둘 다 고기와 생선을 먹었다.)

2 Sally will invite _____ David _____ Jasper to her new house.

(Sally는 David나 Jasper 둘 중 한 명을 그녀의 새 집에 초대할 것이다.)

3 My mom likes _____ coffee _____ tea.

(엄마는 커피뿐만 아니라 차도 좋아하신다.)

4 I ordered _____ a hamburger _____ a steak in the restaurant.

(나는 레스토랑에서 햄버거가 아니라 스테이크를 주문했다.)

5 There was a strong earthquake _____ in Korea _____ in Japan yesterday.

(어제 한국과 일본 두 나라에서 강력한 지진이 발생했다.)

English	Korean	English	Korean
actress	n. 여배우	laugh	v. 웃다
at a very early age	아주 어린 나이에	medicine	n. 의약품
compose	v. 작곡하다	make friends	친구들을 사귀다
during summer vacation	여름 방학 동안에	milk	n. 우유
during winter vacation	겨울 방학 동안에	need	v. 필요로 하다
humid	adj. 습한	school talent show	학교 장기 자랑
juice	n. 쥬스	take a walk	산책하다

🐚 다음의 우리말 표현을 영어로 쓰시오.

1 영어와 스페인어 둘 다
   both English and Spanish
   _____

2 춤을 추거나(dance) 노래를 부르다(sing)
   _____

3 음식과 의약품 둘 다
   _____

4 음식을 먹지도 않았고 친구들을 사귀지도 않았다
   _____

5 우유가 아닌 쥬스를 좋아한다
   _____

6 Sarah의 남편(husband)이 아니라 그녀의 아들(son)
   _____

7 여름 방학 동안이나 겨울 방학 동안에
   _____

8 더울 뿐만 아니라 습한
   _____

9 연주를 했을 뿐만 아니라 작곡도 했다
   _____

10 웃지도 않고 울지도 않다(cry)
   _____

🐚 **다음의 우리말 표현을 영어로 쓰시오.**

1 Sarah는 영어를 말한다.
   ↓
   Sarah speaks English.
   주어   동사   목적어

2 Mike는 춤을 출 것이다 .

_____

3 사람들은 음식을 필요로 한다 .

_____

4 Greg는 음식을 먹었다 .

_____

5 그녀는 우유를 좋아한다 .

_____

6 Sarah의 남편이 장미 몇 송이를 (some roses) 샀다 .

_____

7 David는 여름 방학 동안에 그의 할머니를 방문했다 .

_____

8 낮은 (the days) 너무 (too) 덥다 (hot).

_____

9 Mozart는 피아노를 연주했다 .

_____

10 그 여배우는 웃는다 .

_____

🐚 **다음의 우리말 표현을 영어로 쓰시오.**

1 Sarah는 영어와 스페인어 둘 다를 말한다.

   Sarah speaks both English and Spanish .
   _____

2 Mike는 춤을 추거나 노래를 부를 것이다 .

   _____

3 사람들은 음식과 의약품 둘 다를 필요로 한다.

   _____

4 Greg는 음식을 먹지도 않았고 친구들을 사귀지도 않았다 .

   _____

5 그녀는 우유가 아닌 쥬스를 좋아한다 .

   _____

6 Sarah의 남편이 아니라 그녀의 아들이 장미 몇 송이를 샀다.

   _____

7 David는 여름 방학 동안이나 겨울 방학 동안에 그의 할머니를 방문했다.

   _____

8 낮은 너무 더울 뿐만 아니라 너무 습하다 .

   _____

9 Mozart는 피아노를 연주했을 뿐만 아니라 음악 작곡도 하였다 .

   _____

10 그 여배우는 웃지도 않고 울지도 않는다 .

   _____

🐚 **다음의 우리말 표현을 영어로 쓰시오.**

1 Sarah는 국제 회의에서 영어와 스페인어 둘 다를 말한다.

Sarah speaks both English and Spanish at the international meeting .

2 Mike는 학교 장기 자랑을 위해 춤을 추거나 노래를 부를 것이다.

_____

3 사람들은 생존을 위해 (for survival) 음식과 의약품 둘 다를 필요로 한다.

_____

4 Greg는 그 파티에서 (at the party) 음식을 먹지도 않았고 친구들을 사귀지도 않았다.

_____

5 그녀는 아침 시리얼에 (on her breakfast cereal) 우유가 아닌 쥬스를 좋아한다.

_____

6 Sarah의 남편이 아니라 그녀의 아들이 그녀의 생일선물로 (for her birthday gift) 장미 몇 송이를 샀다.

_____

7 David는 여름 방학 동안이나 겨울 방학 동안에 런던에 있는 (in London) 할머니를 방문했다.

_____

8 낮은 산책 하기에 너무 더울 뿐만 아니라 너무 습하다.

_____

9 Mozart는 아주 어린 나이에 피아노를 연주했을 뿐만 아니라 음악 작곡도 하였다.

_____

10 그 여배우는 그 영화에서 (in the movie) 웃지도 않고 울지도 않는다.

_____

현재완료 1 (계속, 완료)

 Writing에 필요한 문법

1. 현재완료 시제의 형태

주어	have/has	동사의 과거분사(p.p)
I	have	studied.
You / We / They	have	studied.
He / She / It	has	studied.

2. 현재완료 시제 문장 맛보기

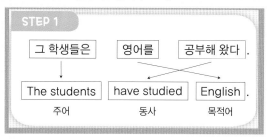

STEP 1

| 그 학생들은 | 영어를 | 공부해 왔다 . |

| The students | have studied | English . |
| 주어 | 동사 | 목적어 |

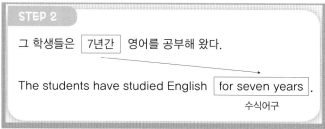

STEP 2

그 학생들은 7년간 영어를 공부해 왔다.

The students have studied English for seven years .
수식어구

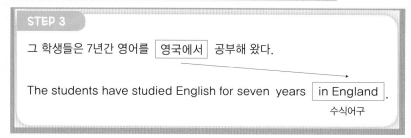

STEP 3

그 학생들은 7년간 영어를 영국에서 공부해 왔다.

The students have studied English for seven years in England .
수식어구

3. 현재완료 시제의 쓰임

쓰임	예문	해석
계속 ① 과거에 시작해서 현재까지 계속 진행 중인 동작이나 상태를 표현할 때 ② for＋기간/since＋시점과 함께 쓰인다.	Steve has stayed in London for three months.	계속해서 -해 왔다
완료 ① 과거에 시작하여 방금 전에 완료된 동작을 표현할 때 ② just, already, yet 등의 부사와 함께 쓰인다.	I have just finished my homework.	방금 -했다

참조

과거에 이미 끝난 동작이나 상태를 표현할 때는 과거 시제를 사용한다.
Steve stayed in London last month.
* 과거시제를 나타내는 부사(구): yesterday, last night, ago, in the past, in＋과거년도

4. 현재완료 시제의 기본 문장

종류	형태	예문
긍정문	주어＋have/has＋과거분사~.	I have eaten Thai food.
부정문	주어＋have/has＋not＋과거분사~.	I have not eaten Thai food.
의문문	Have/Has＋주어＋과거분사~?	Have you eaten Thai food?

* have not=haven't   has not=hasn't

🐺 Writing에 필요한 문법 확인

A. 다음 중 알맞은 것을 고르시오.

1 Justin (went / has gone) to the science museum last summer vacation.

2 Brian (teaches / has taught) math for two months.

3 The students (have studied / studied) hard for the test last week.

4 Jason (learned / has learned) French since 2016.

5 They (knew / have known) each other for five years.

B. 주어진 동사를 이용하여 문장을 완성하시오.

1 Justin _____ to Nepal last winter. (move)

2 Mike _____ already _____ breakfast. (eat)

3 They _____ for the test since yesterday. (prepare)

4 It _____ a lot last month. (rain)

5 The students _____ the book yet. (not, read)

Warm Up : 표현 만들기

English	Korean	English	Korean
collect	v. 수집하다	result	n. 결과
difficulty	n. 어려움	save	v. 구하다
firefighter	n. 소방관	statue	n. 조각상
large-scale	adj. 큰 규모의	the homeless	n. 노숙자들
life	n. 생명, 목숨	valuable	adj. 소중한
poverty	n. 가난	volunteer	n. 자원봉사자
provide	v. 제공하다	warn	v. 경고하다

🐚 다음의 우리말 표현을 영어로 쓰시오.

1 그 학생들은 공부해 왔다   The students have studied _____

2 사람들은 써왔다(write) _____

3 자원봉사자들은 제공해 왔다 _____

4 과학자들은 경고해 왔다 _____

5 그는 만들어 왔다(work on) _____

6 그들은 살아왔다 _____

7 Mike는 만들어 왔다(build) _____

8 소방관들은 구해 왔다 _____

9 그들은 수집해 왔다 _____

10 Jason은 만나왔다(meet) _____

🐚 **다음의 우리말 표현을 영어로 쓰시오.**

1 그 학생들은　영어를　공부해 왔다.

The students　have studied　English.
　주어　　　　　동사　　　　목적어

2 사람들은　책들을　써왔다 .

_____

3 자원봉사자들은　음식을　제공해 왔다 .

_____

4 과학자들은　우리에게　경고해 왔다 .

_____

5 그는　그 조각상을　만들어 왔다 .

_____

6 그들은　도시에 (a city)　살아왔다 .

_____

7 Mike는　웹사이트를 (a website)　만들어 왔다 .

_____

8 소방관들은　생명들을　구해 왔다 .

_____

9 그들은　책들을　수집해 왔다 .

_____

10 Jason은　사람들을　만나왔다 .

_____

🐚 **다음의 우리말 표현을 영어로 쓰시오.**

1 그 학생들은 ⬜7년간⬜ 영어를 공부해 왔다.

The students have studied English _for seven years_ .

2 사람들은 ⬜심각한 문제들에 대한⬜ (about the serious problems) 책들을 써왔다.

_____

3 자원봉사자들은 ⬜노숙자들에게⬜ 음식을 제공해 왔다.

_____

4 과학자들은 우리에게 ⬜대기 오염에 대해⬜ (about air pollution) 경고해 왔다.

_____

5 그는 ⬜거대한⬜ (huge) 조각상을 만들어 왔다.

_____

6 그들은 ⬜큰⬜ 도시에 살아왔다.

_____

7 Mike는 ⬜큰 규모의⬜ 웹사이트를 만들어 왔다.

_____

8 소방관들은 ⬜소중한⬜ 생명들을 구해 왔다.

_____

9 그들은 ⬜보기 힘든⬜ (rare) 책들을 수집해 왔다.

_____

10 Jason은 ⬜다양한⬜ (various) 사람들을 만나왔다.

_____

🐚 **다음의 우리말 표현을 영어로 쓰시오.**

1 그 학생들은 7년간 영어를 영국에서 공부해 왔다.

   The students have studied English for seven years   in England .

2 사람들은 가난의 심각한 문제들에 대한 책들을 써왔다.

   _____

3 자원봉사자들은 3년 동안 노숙자들에게 음식을 제공해 왔다.

   _____

4 과학자들은 우리에게 대기 오염에 대해 여러 차례 (several times) 경고해 왔다.

   _____

5 그는 거대한 조각상을 10년간 만들어 왔다.

   _____

6 그들은 작년 이래로 큰 도시에 살아왔다.

   _____

7 Mike는 어떠한 어려움 없이 (without any difficulties) 큰 규모의 웹사이트를 만들어
   왔다.

   _____

8 소방관들은 많은 어려움에도 불구하고 (in spite of many difficulties) 소중한 생명들
   을 구해 왔다.

   _____

9 그들은 7년간 보기 힘든 책들을 수집해 왔다.

   _____

10 Jason은 2015년 여름 이래로 (since the summer of 2015) 다양한 사람들을 만나왔다.

   _____

More Practice

A. 주어진 단어를 사용하여 문장을 완성하시오.

1 are / in Europe / both Paris and London / Sally's favorite cities / .

   _____

2 was / neither / at school / last Monday / nor at home / Peter / .

   _____

3 not only / David / plays the piano / but also plays the flute well / .

   _____

4 at the pool / has swum / for one hour / Sam / .

   _____

B. 다음 문장을 영작하시오.

1 David는 작년부터 그의 할머니의 정원에 있는 화초들에 물을 줘 왔다. (water, in his grandmother's garden)

   _____

2 Jake 뿐만 아니라 Greg도 큰 장난감 가게에서 새로운 장난감을 샀다. (in the big toy store)

   _____

3 Drake는 영국 역사에 대한 20권이 넘는 책을 써 왔다. (about the history of England)

   _____

4 James는 이미 두 개의 작문 코스를 성공적으로 끝냈다. (with success)

   _____

Creative Thinking Activity

🐚 다음 표를 보고 각 인물들이 해 온 일을 문장으로 묘사하시오.

	Years	Job
Brian	2009-now	working for Orange Ads
Justin	2010-now	studying drawing at NY Art School
Ken	2011-now	teaching Italian
James	2012-now	creating advertisements for Pear Company
Jack	2013-now	writing novels for children

1 Brian has worked for Orange Ads since 2009.

2 Justin _____ .

3 Ken _____ .

4 James _____ .

5 Jack _____ .

현재완료 2 (경험, 결과)

 Writing에 필요한 문법

1. 현재완료 시제의 형태

주어	have/has	과거분사
I	have	studied.
You / We / They	have	studied.
He / She / It	has	studied.

2. 현재완료 시제 문장 맛보기

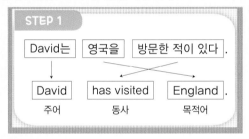

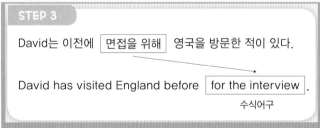

3. 현재완료 시제의 쓰임

쓰임	예문	해석
경험 ① 이전부터 현재까지 경험해 본 일을 표현할 때 ② before, once, several times, ever, never 등과 함께 쓰인다.	Brian has been in London before.	–한 적이 있다
결과 과거에 일어난 어떤 일이 현재까지 영향을 미치고 있음을 표현할 때	Brian has gone to London.	(과거에) –했다 (그래서 현재 –한 상태이다)

🦫 Writing에 필요한 문법 확인

A. 다음 중 틀린 부분을 바르게 고치시오.

1. I seen the movie twice before.
   _____

2. Have she tried Vietnamese food?
   _____

3. The students never read the book in French before.
   _____

4. I have see a shooting star before.
   _____

5. Brian has invite Sam several times.
   _____

B. 주어진 동사를 이용하여 현재 완료시제 문장을 완성하시오.

1. _____ you _____ the science teacher before? (meet)

2. _____ Mike _____ lunch at the famous café? (have)

3. Justin _____ _____ _____ in Paris. (never, live)

4. They _____ _____ to the new student once. (talk)

5. Mom _____ _____ the oven twice. (use)

C. 보기의 동사를 이용하여 문장을 완성하시오.

보기				
work	take	see	be	finish

1. _____ you _____ David's new film? (David의 새 영화를 본 적 있니?)

2. Jacob _____ _____ _____ the homework on time.
   (Jacob은 결코 제 시간에 숙제를 끝낸 적이 없다.)

3. I _____ _____ at a restaurant near the school.
   (나는 학교 근처의 식당에서 일을 한 적이 있다.)

4. How many times _____ she _____ _____ London?
   (얼마나 많이 그녀는 런던에 가 본적이 있니?)

5. _____ Jason _____ riding lessons? (Jason은 승마를 배운 적이 있니?)

English	Korean	English	Korean
active	adj. 활동적인	powerful	adj. 강력한
break	v. 부러지다	reach the semifinals	준결승에 진출하다
broken	adj. 고장난	restaurant	n. 식당
by hand	손으로	short story	단편 소설
fix	v. 고치다	sick	adj. 아픈
leg	n. 다리	sneakers	n. 운동화
paint blue	파랑 색으로 칠하다	wash	v. (옷 등을) 세탁하다

다음의 우리말 표현을 영어로 쓰시오.

1 David는 방문한 적이 있다   David has visited

2 그 아이들은 본 적이 없다(see)

3 Jacob은 칠해본 적이 있다

4 그 한국팀은 진출한 적이 있다(reach)

5 Mike는 고쳐 본 적이 있다(repair)

6 그 소년은 부러진 적이 있다

7 Ken은 세탁해 본 적이 있다

8 나는 배운 적이 있다(learn)

9 Brian은 만든 적이 있다(make)

10 Peter는 써 본 적이 있다(write)

🐚 **다음의 우리말 표현을 영어로 쓰시오.**

1　David는　영국을　방문한 적이 있다.

　　↓

　　David　has visited　England.
　　주어　　　동사　　　목적어

2　그 아이들은　눈을 (snow)　본 적이 없다 .

　　_____

3　Jacob은　그의 침실을 (his bedroom)　칠해본 적이 있다 .

　　_____

4　그 한국팀은　준결승에　진출한 적이 있다 .

　　_____

5　Mike는　자동차들을　고쳐 본 적이 있다 .

　　_____

6　그 소년은　다리가　부러진 적이 있다 .

　　_____

7　Ken은　그의 운동화를　세탁해 본 적이 있다 .

　　_____

8　나는　미식축구를 (football)　배운 적이 있다 .

　　_____

9　Brian은　음식을　만든 적이 있다 .

　　_____

10　Peter는　단편 소설들을　써 본 적이 있다 .

　　_____

🐚 **다음의 우리말 표현을 영어로 쓰시오.**

1 David는 이전에 영국을 방문한 적이 있다.

David has visited England   before .

_____

2 그 아이들은 눈을 본 적이 결코 (never) 없다.

_____

3 Jacob은 그의 침실을 파랑 색으로 칠해본 적이 있다.

_____

4 그 한국팀은 월드컵 (of the World Cup) 준결승에 진출한 적이 있다.

_____

5 Mike는 고장난 자동차들을 고쳐 본 적이 있다.

_____

6 그 소년은 다리가 부러진 적이 세 번 (three times) 있다.

_____

7 Ken은 그의 운동화를 손으로 세탁해 본 적이 있다.

_____

8 나는 David로부터 (from David) 미식축구를 배운 적이 있다.

_____

9 Brian은 특별한 (special) 음식을 만든 적이 있다.

_____

10 Peter는 어린 아이들을 위한 (for young children) 단편 소설들을 써 본 적이 있다.

_____

🐚 **다음의 우리말 표현을 영어로 쓰시오.**

1 David는 이전에 면접을 위해 영국을 방문한 적이 있다.

   David has visited England before for the interview .

2 아프리카에 있는 (in Africa) 그 아이들은 눈을 본 적이 결코 없다.

   _____

3 Jacob은 그의 침실을 파랑 색으로 칠해본 적이 세 번 (three times) 있다.

   _____

4 그 한국팀은 월드컵 준결승에 진출한 적이 한 번 (once) 있다.

   _____

5 Mike는 고장난 자동차들을 여러 번 (several times) 고쳐 본 적이 있다.

   _____

6 그 활동적인 소년은 다리가 부러진 적이 세 번 있다.

   _____

7 Ken은 그의 운동화를 손으로 세탁해 본 적이 두 번 (twice) 있다.

   _____

8 나는 미국에서 (in America) David로부터 미식축구를 배운 적이 있다.

   _____

9 Brian은 그의 아픈 엄마를 위해 특별한 음식을 만든 적이 있다.

   _____

10 Peter는 예전에 (before) 어린 아이들을 위한 단편 소설들을 써 본 적이 있다.

   _____

Unit 5 지각동사

Writing에 필요한 문법

1. 지각동사란?

- 보고, 듣고, 느끼고, 맛보는 등의 감각을 나타내는 동사
- see, hear, feel, smell 등
- 목적격보어로 동사원형 또는 분사를 쓴다.

2. 지각동사가 있는 문장 맛보기

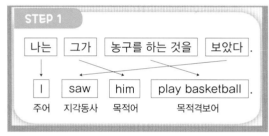

STEP 1

| 나는 | 그가 | 농구를 하는 것을 | 보았다 |

| I | saw | him | play basketball |
| 주어 | 지각동사 | 목적어 | 목적격보어 |

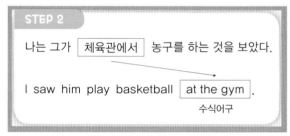

STEP 2

나는 그가 체육관에서 농구를 하는 것을 보았다.

I saw him play basketball at the gym.
수식어구

STEP 3

나는 어제 그가 체육관에서 농구를 하는 것을 보았다.

I saw him play basketball at the gym yesterday.
부사

3. 지각동사의 쓰임

쓰임	예문
주어가 목적어의 활동을 지각했을 때: 주어+지각동사+목적어+동사원형~.	I heard a famous singer sing at the concert yesterday.
주어가 목적어의 활동을 지각했을 당시, 그 활동이 진행중인 것을 강조할 때: 주어+지각동사+목적어+현재분사(V-ing)~.	I heard Mom singing a song in the living room.
목적어의 활동을 지각했을 당시, 그 활동이 수동적일 때: 주어+지각동사+목적어+과거분사(p.p)~.	I heard my name called.

4. 지각동사 vs. 감각동사

	지각동사	예문	감각동사	예문
시각	see, watch, look at, notice	I didn't see you come in.	look	You look good.
청각	hear, listen to	I heard the baby crying.	sound	That song sounds peaceful.
촉각	feel	She felt someone touch her shoulder.	feel	I feel tired.
미각	smell	I smell something burning.	smell	The pizza smells delicious.

🐦 Writing에 필요한 문법 확인

A. 다음 중 알맞은 것을 고르시오.

1 The cake smells (good / well).

2 The movie looks (interested / interesting).

3 I saw my neighbor (go / to go) somewhere.

4 He felt someone (tap / to tap) his back.

5 She didn't hear her dog (come / to come) to the bedroom.

B. 다음 중 틀린 부분을 고르시오.

1 He watched her to walk down the road.
    ⓐ   ⓑ   ⓒ   ⓓ

2 I saw her cleaned the room.
    ⓐ ⓑ   ⓒ   ⓓ

3 The song sounds very calmly.
    ⓐ   ⓑ   ⓒ   ⓓ

4 You saw me to dance.
    ⓐ ⓑ ⓒ   ⓓ

5 I heard you to play a famous song.
    ⓐ ⓑ ⓒ   ⓓ

C. 주어진 단어를 사용하여 문장을 완성하시오.

1 bark / heard / he / my dogs / .

_____

2 good / smells / the muffin / .

_____

3 heard / you / I / talk on the phone / .

_____

 Warm Up : 표현 만들기

English	Korean	English	Korean
above	adv. -보다 위에	horizon	n. 수평선, 지평선
bamboo	n. 대나무	kitchen counter	부엌 조리대
boil	v. (물이나 액체 등이) 끓다	meow	v. 고양이가 야옹 울다
bug	n. 벌레	neighbor	n. 이웃
carefully	adv. 주의하여	rise	v. (해 등이) 떠오르다
crawl	v. (벌레, 곤충이) 기어가다	snack	n. 간식
gym	n. 체육관	wash the dishes	설거지를 하다

🐚 **다음의 우리말 표현을 영어로 쓰시오.**

1 그를 보았다(see)   saw him _____

2 해를 보았다(look at)   _____

3 나의 고양이들을 들었다(hear) _____

4 그들의 선생님을 들었다(listen to) _____

5 그녀의 강아지를 느꼈다(feel) _____

6 물을 들었다(hear)   _____

7 어떤 벌레를 느꼈다(feel)   _____

8 그의 아빠를 보았다(see)   _____

9 무엇인가를 냄새맡았다(smell, something) _____

10 판다들을 보았다(watch, some pandas) _____

◎ 다음의 우리말 표현을 영어로 쓰시오.

1 나는 그가 농구를 하는 것을 보았다.

　I saw him play basketball.
　주어　동사　목적어　　목적격보어

2 그녀는 해가 떠오르고 있는 것을 (rising) 보았다 .

_____

3 나는 나의 고양이들이 야옹 우는 것을 들었다 .

_____

4 그들은 그들의 선생님이 기말 시험에 대해서 말하는 것을 (the final exam)
　들었다 (listen to).

_____

5 그녀는 그녀의 강아지가 그녀에게 오고 있는 것을 (coming to) 느꼈다 .

_____

6 엄마는 물이 끓고 있는 소리를 (boiling) 들었다 .

_____

7 나는 벌레가 나의 몸에 기어가는 것을 (on my body) 느꼈다 .

_____

8 그는 그의 아빠가 설거지를 하는 것을 보았다 .

_____

9 나는 무엇인가가 요리되고 있는 (cooking) 냄새를 맡았다 .

_____

10 그 소년은 판다들이 대나무를 먹는 것을 보았다 (watch).

_____

🐚 **다음의 우리말 표현을 영어로 쓰시오.**

1 나는 그가 `체육관에서` 농구를 하는 것을 보았다.

I saw him play basketball   at the gym .

2 그녀는 `지평선에서` (from the horizon) 해가 떠오르고 있는 것을 보았다.

3 나는 나의 고양이들이 `크게` (loudly) 야옹 우는 것을 들었다.

4 그들은 그들의 선생님이 기말 시험에 대해서 말하는 것을 `주의하여` 들었다.

5 그녀는 그녀의 강아지가 그녀에게 `더 가까이` (closer) 오고 있는 것을 느꼈다.

6 엄마는 `냄비에서` (in the pot) 물이 끓고 있는 소리를 들었다.

7 나는 `숲에서` (in the forest) 벌레가 나의 몸에 기어가는 것을 느꼈다.

8 그는 그의 아빠가 `간식을 먹은 후에` (after a snack) 설거지를 하는 것을 보았다.

9 나는 `부엌에서` (in the kitchen) 무엇인가가 요리되고 있는 냄새를 맡았다.

10 그 소년은 판다들이 `많은 양의` (a lot of) 대나무를 먹는 것을 보았다.

🍡 다음의 우리말 표현을 영어로 쓰시오.

1 나는 어제 그가 체육관에서 농구를 하는 것을 보았다.

I saw him play basketball at the gym yesterday.

_____

2 그녀는 산 위의 (above the mountain) 지평선에서 해가 떠오르고 있는 것을 보았다.

_____

3 나는 침실에서 (in the bedroom) 나의 고양이들이 크게 야옹 우는 것을 들었다.

_____

4 그들은 수업 시간에 (in class) 그들의 선생님이 기말 시험에 대해서 말하는 것을 주의하여 들었다.

_____

5 그녀는 침대 위에서 (on the bed) 그녀의 강아지가 그녀에게 더 가까이 오고 있는 것을 느꼈다.

_____

6 엄마는 부엌 조리대의 (on the kitchen counter) 냄비에서 물이 끓고 있는 소리를 들었다.

_____

7 나는 몇 분 전에 (a few minutes ago) 숲에서 벌레가 나의 몸에 기어가는 것을 느꼈다.

_____

8 그는 지난 밤에 (last night) 그의 아빠가 간식을 먹은 후에 설거지를 하는 것을 보았다.

_____

9 나는 이웃집 (from my neighbor's house) 부엌에서 무엇인가가 요리되고 있는 냄새를 맡았다.

_____

10 그 소년은 동물원에서 (at the zoo) 판다들이 많은 양의 대나무를 먹는 것을 보았다.

_____

수동태

Writing에 필요한 문법

1. 수동태의 형태

| be동사+과거분사 | I · feed · my dog . (능동태)
 My dog · is fed · by me . (수동태) |

2. 수동태 문장 맛보기

STEP 1

그 상자들은 │ Brian에 의해서 │ 옮겨졌다 .

The boxes │ were moved │ by Brian .
주어 · 동사

STEP 2

그 │ 무거운 │ 상자들은 Brian에 의해서 옮겨졌다.

The │ heavy │ boxes were moved by Brian.
형용사

STEP 3

그 무거운 상자들은 │ 2시간 전에 │ Brian에 의해서 옮겨졌다.

The heavy boxes were moved by Brian │ two hours ago │.
수식어구

3. 수동태의 쓰임

쓰임	예문	해석
주어가 동작이나 행위를 당하는 것을 표현할 때	The bicycle is repaired by my father.	-하여지다, -당하다

4. 수동태의 기본 문장

종류	형태	예문
긍정문	주어+be+과거분사+by+행위주체자~.	The photo was taken by Jinsu.
부정문	주어+be+not+과거분사+by+행위주체자~.	The photo was not taken by Jinsu.
의문문	Be+주어+과거분사+by+행위주체자?	Was the photo taken by Jinsu?

5. 시제에 따른 수동태 변화

시제	예문
현재	Dinner is cooked by Mom.
과거	Dinner was cooked by Mom.
미래	Dinner will(is going to) be cooked by Mom.
현재진행	Dinner is being cooked by Mom.
과거진행	Dinner was being cooked by Mom.
현재완료	Dinner has been cooked by Mom.

🔊 Writing에 필요한 문법 확인

A. 다음 중 알맞은 것을 고르시오.

1 My name (writes / is written) on the paper.

2 The picture (painted / was painted) by Karen.

3 John (taught / was taught) English by Mrs. White.

4 They usually (eat / are eaten) some fruit after meals.

5 We (will hold / will be held) an art exhibition next weekend.

B. 밑줄 친 부분을 바르게 고치시오.

1 My watch repairs by Jason.

2 The picture were painted last year by my sister.

3 The furniture will moved tomorrow by my brother.

4 The apples was eaten last night by the children.

5 She was bitten to a mosquito.

C. 다음 능동태 문장을 수동태 문장으로 바꿔 쓰시오.

1 My brother is fixing a computer.

_____

2   I broke the window yesterday.   _____

3   The police caught the thief.   _____

4   They read the comic book.   _____

5   Susan and her sister played the computer game.

_____

English	Korean	English	Korean
explain	v. 설명하다	serve	v. 제공하다
finish	v. 끝내다	suggest	v. 제안하다
foreign	adj. 외국의	teach	v. 가르치다
idea	n. 아이디어, 생각	theory	n. 이론
invite	v. 초대하다	turn on	(라디오 등을) 켜다
language	n. 언어	waiter	n. 웨이터, 종업원
professor	n. 교수	write	n. 쓰다

다음의 우리말 표현을 영어로 쓰시오.

1   그 상자들은 옮겨졌다   The boxes were moved

2   그 이야기는 쓰여지지 않았다   _____

3   집이 지어질 것이다   _____

4   나는 초대 되었다   _____

5   그 일은 끝나지 않을 것이다   _____

6   그 이론은 설명되고 있다   _____

7   그 라디오는 켜진다   _____

8   그 음식은 제공된다   _____

9   언어들이 가르쳐진다   _____

10 그 아이디어는 제안되었다   _____

🐚 다음의 우리말 표현을 영어로 쓰시오.

1 그 상자들은 Brian에 의해서 옮겨졌다.

   The boxes were moved by Brian.
   주어   동사

2 그 이야기는   Jay에 의해서   쓰여지지 않았다 .

   _____

3 집이   나의 아버지에 의해서   지어질 것이다 .

   _____

4 나는   나의 친구에 의해서   초대되었다 .

   _____

5 그 일은   그들에 의해서   끝나지 않을 것이다 .

   _____

6 그 이론은   나의 교수님에 의해서   설명되고 있다 .

   _____

7 그 라디오는   나에 의해서   켜진다 .

   _____

8 그 음식은   그 웨이터에 의해서   제공된다 .

   _____

9 언어들이   선생님들에 의해서   가르쳐진다 .

   _____

10 그 아이디어는   나의 부모님에 의해서   제안되었다 .

   _____

다음의 우리말 표현을 영어로 쓰시오.

1 그 무거운 상자들은 Brian에 의해서 옮겨졌다.

   The heavy boxes were moved by Brian.

   _____

2 그 슬픈 (sad) 이야기는 Jay에 의해서 쓰여지지 않았다.

   _____

3 큰 (big) 집이 나의 아버지에 의해서 지어질 것이다.

   _____

4 나는 나의 가장 친한 (best) 친구에 의해서 초대되었다.

   _____

5 그 어려운 (hard) 일은 그들에 의해서 끝나지 않을 것이다.

   _____

6 그 새로운 이론은 나의 교수님에 의해서 설명되고 있다.

   _____

7 그 빨강색 라디오는 나에 의해서 켜진다.

   _____

8 그 음식은 그 키가 큰 웨이터에 의해서 제공된다.

   _____

9 외국의 언어들이 선생님들에 의해서 가르쳐진다.

   _____

10 그 좋은 (good) 아이디어는 나의 부모님에 의해서 제안되었다.

   _____

🐚 **다음의 우리말 표현을 영어로 쓰시오.**

1 그 무거운 상자들은   2시간 전에   Brian에 의해서 옮겨졌다.

   The heavy boxes were moved by Brian   two hours ago .
   _____

2 그 슬픈 이야기는   2010년에   Jay에 의해서 쓰여지지 않았다.

   _____

3 큰 집이   내년에   나의 아버지에 의해서 지어질 것이다.

   _____

4 나는 나의 가장 친한 친구에 의해서   결혼식에 (to the wedding) 초대되었다.

   _____

5 그 어려운 일은 그들에 의해서   제 시간에 (on time) 끝나지 않을 것이다.

   _____

6 그 새로운 이론은   세미나에서 (at the seminar) 나의 교수님에 의해서 설명되고 있다.

   _____

7 그 빨강색 라디오는   매일 밤 (every night) 나에 의해서 켜진다.

   _____

8 그 음식은   음식점에서 (at the restaurant) 그 키 큰 웨이터에 의해서 제공된다.

   _____

9 외국의 언어들이   학교에서 (at school) 선생님들에 의해서 가르쳐진다.

   _____

10 그 좋은 아이디어는   지난 달에   나의 부모님에 의해서 제안되었다.

   _____

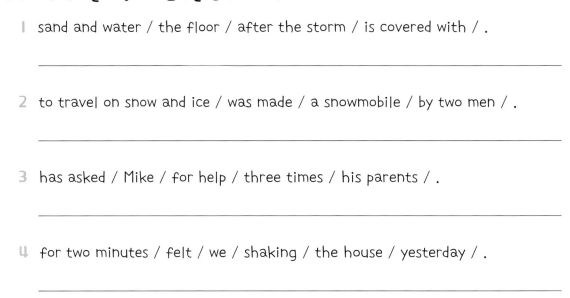

More Practice

A. 주어진 단어를 사용하여 문장을 완성하시오.

1 sand and water / the floor / after the storm / is covered with / .

_____

2 to travel on snow and ice / was made / a snowmobile / by two men / .

_____

3 has asked / Mike / for help / three times / his parents / .

_____

4 for two minutes / felt / we / shaking / the house / yesterday / .

_____

B. 다음 문장을 영작하시오.

1 나는 전에 중국 음식과 태국 음식 둘 다를 식당에서 먹어본 적이 없다. (both Chinese and Thai food)

_____

2 런던에서 온 이 영리한 개는 세계 개 대회에서 두 번 상을 받은 적이 있다. (win the award in a world dog competition)

_____

3 그 유명한 희곡 Romeo and Juliet은 J. K. Rowling에 의해 쓰여진 것이 아니라 William Shakespeare에 의해 쓰여졌다. (the famous play)

_____

4 나는 그 영리한 개가 그의 가족을 여러 가지로 돕는 것을 보았다. (in many ways)

_____

🐚 다음 표를 보고 각 인물들이 했던 일을 수동태 문장으로 묘사하시오.

Name	Verb	Work of Art
J. K. Rowling	write	*Harry Potter* series
Gustave Eiffel	build	Eiffel Tower
Charlie Chaplin	make	the film Modern Times
Pablo Picasso	paint	*The Weeping Woman*
Amadeus Mozart	compose	the opera *Don Giovanni*

[보기] The picture was taken by Rob.

1 _____

2 _____

3 _____

4 _____

5 _____

Unit 7 조동사 can, may

 Writing에 필요한 문법

1. 조동사 can과 may의 형태

– 인칭에 상관없이 같은 형태를 갖는다.
– can과 may 뒤에는 동사원형을 쓴다.

주어	조동사	동사원형
I		
You / We / They	can / may	swim.
He / She / It		

2. 조동사 can이 있는 문장 맛보기

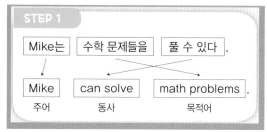

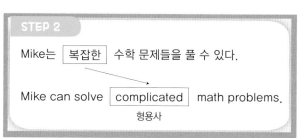

STEP 3

Mike는 [어려움 없이] 복잡한 수학 문제들을 풀 수 있다.

Mike can solve complicated math problems [without difficulty].
수식어구

3. 조동사 can과 may의 쓰임

	예문	해석
can	He can swim in the lake.	-할 수 있다 (능력, 가능)
	Can I use your cellphone?	-해도 된다 (허락)
may	May I get some paper?	-해도 된다 (허락)
	He may be busy.	-일지도 모른다 (추측)

4. 조동사 can과 may의 기본 문장

종류	형태	예문
긍정문	주어＋can/may＋동사원형~.	I can read the book. I may read the book.
부정문	주어＋cannot/may not＋동사원형~.	I cannot read the book. I may not read the book.
의문문	Can/May＋주어＋동사원형~?	Can you read the book? May I read the book?

* can의 과거형은 could

5. 조동사 can과 be able to의 쓰임

can이 능력이나 가능의 의미로 쓰일 때 be able to로 바꿔 쓸 수 있다.

주어	be able to			동사원형
	과거(-할 수 있었다)	현재(-할 수 있다)	미래(-할 수 있을 것이다)	
I	was able to	am able to	will be able to	swim.
You/We/They	were able to	are able to		
He/She/It	was able to	is able to		

🐾 Writing에 필요한 문법 확인

A. 다음 중 틀린 부분을 바르게 고치시오.

1 He may fails the final exam. _____

2 Billy can't finish the project last week. _____

3 Jason can drove the car next month. _____

4 The children couldn't saw the box because the room had no light. _____

5 Can he speaks French in class? _____

B. 주어진 동사를 이용하여 문장을 완성하시오.

1 Sophia _____ tomorrow. (go hiking)
(Sophia는 내일 하이킹을 갈지도 모른다.)

2 _____ I _____ the reason of your absence? (ask)

(왜 결석했는지 물어봐도 될까요?)

3 You _____ in the museum. (take pictures)

(당신은 박물관 안에서 사진을 찍을 수 없습니다.)

4 Jacob _____ the money because he lent it to David. (save)

(Jacob은 그의 돈을 David에게 빌려주어서 저축할 수 없었다.)

5 We _____ in heavy rain. (play soccer)

(우리는 폭우에는 축구를 할 수 없다.)

 Warm Up : 표현 만들기

English	Korean	English	Korean
accident	n. 사고	overcome	v. 극복하다
cause	n. 원인	poisonous	adj. 독이 있는
challenging	adj. 도전적인	prove	v. 증명하다
complain of	-을/를 호소하다, 불평하다	provide	v. 제공하다
completely	adv. 완전히	spoiled	adj. 상한
finally	adv. 마침내	stomachache	n. 복통
graduate from	-을/를 졸업하다	talented	adj. 재능 있는

🐚 **다음의 우리말 표현을 영어로 쓰시오.**

1 Mike는 풀 수 있다   Mike can solve

2 그는 졸업할 수 있다

3 그녀는 끝낼 수 없을지도 모른다

4 그들은 제공할 수 없었다

5 뱀은 죽일 수 있다

6 Cooper는 증명할 수 있었다

7 그녀의 아들은 연주할 수 있었다

8 학생들이 호소할지도 모른다

9 그는 극복할지도 모른다

10 나는 저축할 수 있었다

🐚 **다음의 우리말 표현을 영어로 쓰시오.**

1 Mike는 수학 문제들을 풀 수 있다.

    Mike   can solve   math problems.
     주어   동사   목적어

2 그는   대학교를 (university)   졸업할 수 있다 .

_____

3 그녀는   그 역사 과제를 (the history project)   끝낼 수 없을지도 모른다 .

_____

4 그들은   음식을   제공할 수 없었다 .

_____

5 뱀은   너를   죽일 수 있다 .

_____

6 Cooper는   그 사고의 원인을 (the cause of the accident)   증명할 수 있었다 .

_____

7 그녀의 아들은   바이올린을   연주할 수 있었다 .

_____

8 학생들이   복통들을   호소할지도 모른다 .

_____

9 그는   그 어려움을   극복할지도 모른다 .

_____

10 나는   돈을   저축할 수 있었다 .

_____

🐚 **다음의 우리말 표현을 영어로 쓰시오.**

1 Mike는 [복잡한] 수학 문제들을 풀 수 있다.

    Mike can solve complicated math problems.

    _____

2 그는 대학교를 [올 해에] 졸업할 수 있다.

    _____

3 그녀는 그 [도전적인] 역사 과제를 끝낼 수 없을지도 모른다.

    _____

4 그들은 [충분한] 음식을 제공할 수 없었다.

    _____

5 [독이 있는] 뱀은 너를 죽일 수 있다.

    _____

6 Cooper는 그 사고의 원인을 [명백하게] (clearly) 증명할 수 있었다.

    _____

7 그녀의 [재능 있는] 아들은 바이올린을 연주할 수 있었다.

    _____

8 [이 학교에 있는] (in this school) 학생들이 복통들을 호소할지도 모른다.

    _____

9 그는 그 어려움을 [완전히] 극복할지도 모른다.

    _____

10 나는 [많은] 돈을 저축할 수 있었다.

    _____

🐚 다음의 우리말 표현을 영어로 쓰시오.

1. Mike는 어려움 없이 복잡한 수학 문제들을 풀 수 있다.

   Mike can solve complicated math problems without difficulty .

2. 그는 마침내 대학교를 올 해에 졸업할 수 있다.

   _____

3. 그녀는 그 도전적인 역사 과제를 제 시간에 (on time) 끝낼 수 없을지도 모른다.

   _____

4. 그들은 노숙자들에게 (to the homeless) 충분한 음식을 제공할 수 없었다.

   _____

5. 독이 있는 뱀은 너를 순식간에 (in an instant) 죽일 수 있다.

   _____

6. 정부 덕분에 (thanks to government), Cooper는 그 사고의 원인을 명백하게 증명할 수 있었다.

   _____

7. 그녀의 재능 있는 아들은 2살 때 (at the age of two) 바이올린을 연주할 수 있었다.

   _____

8. 상한 우유 때문에 이 학교에 있는 학생들이 복통들을 호소할지도 모른다.

   _____

9. 그는 그 어려움을 긍정적인 태도로 (with a positive attitude) 완전히 극복할지도 모른다.

   _____

10. 나는 부모님의 도움 없이 (without help from my parents) 많은 돈을 저축할 수 있었다.

    _____

조동사 should, had better

 Writing에 필요한 문법

1. 조동사 should와 had better의 형태
- 인칭에 따른 변화없이 동일한 형태를 갖는다.
- should와 had better 뒤에는 동사원형을 쓴다.

주어	조동사	동사원형
I	should had better	start.
You / We / They		
He / She / It		

2. 조동사 should가 있는 문장 맛보기

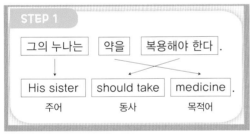

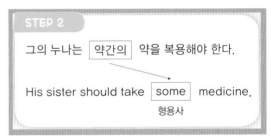

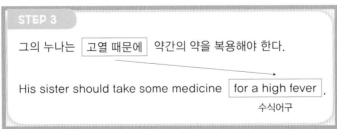

3. 조동사 should와 had better의 쓰임

쓰임	예문	해석
충고나 제안을 할 때	You should help your friends.	-해야 한다
	We had better leave for Busan now.	-하는 것이 좋겠다

4. 조동사 should와 had better의 기본 문장

종류	형태	예문
긍정문	주어+should/had better+동사원형~.	Jane should clean her room. Jane had better clean her room.
부정문	주어+should/had better+not+동사원형~.	Children should not stay up late. Children had better not stay up late.
의문문	should+주어+동사원형~?	Should we ask for help?

* should not=shouldn't   주어 had better=주어'd better

🐺 Writing에 필요한 문법 확인

A. 주어진 동사와 should 또는 shouldn't를 함께 사용하여 문장을 완성하시오.

1 We _____ our nature for the future. (protect)

2 People _____ the traffic rules. (follow)

3 We _____ the street at a red light. (cross)

4 You _____ a balanced diet for your health. (eat)

5 You _____ outside in the heavy rain. (play)

B. 다음 중 알맞은 것을 고르시오.

1 I'm late for school. I (had better / had better not) hurry up.

2 You (had better / had better not) go in too deep in the pool.

3 It's raining. Tom (has better / had better) take an umbrella.

4 Jane has a meeting soon. She (has better / had better) leave now.

5 Sean has a race tomorrow. He (has better not / had better not) stay up tonight.

C. 다음 중 틀린 부분을 바르게 고치시오.

1 Jake shoulds buy a gift for his friend's birthday. _____

2 You'ad better not play video games today. _____

3 I should cleaned my room after the party. _____

4 They had better studying in the library for the exam. _____

5 Anna had better doesn't eat too many chocolate candies. _____

Warm Up : 표현 만들기

English	Korean	English	Korean
athlete	n. 운동선수	ride	v. (탈 것을) 타다
bicycle	n. 자전거	spicy	adj. 매운
caramel	n. 캐러멜	spot	n. 얼룩
do (one's) homework	v. 숙제를 하다	take	v. (약 등을) 복용하다
medicine	n. 약	take out	(얼룩 등을) 빼내다
play	v. 연주하다	warm	adj. 따뜻한
practice	v. 연습하다	wear	v. 입다

다음의 우리말 표현을 영어로 쓰시오.

1 (약을) 복용해야 한다   should take

2 연습해야 한다 _____

3 숙제를 해야 한다 _____

4 먹으면 안 된다 _____

5 연주하면 안 된다 _____

6 (얼룩을) 빼내는 게 좋겠다 _____

7 가는 게 좋겠다 _____

8 입는 게 좋겠다 _____

9 타지 않는 게 좋겠다 _____

10 먹지 않는 게 좋겠다 _____

🐚 **다음의 우리말 표현을 영어로 쓰시오.**

1.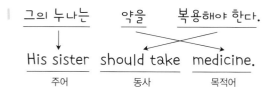

   그의 누나는　약을　복용해야 한다.

   His sister　should take　medicine.
   주어　동사　목적어

2. 그 선수는　달리기를　연습해야 한다 .

   _____

3. 학생들은　그들의 숙제를　해야 한다 .

   _____

4. 어린이들은　캐러멜들을　먹으면 안 된다 .

   _____

5. 우리는　음악을　연주하면 안 된다 .

   _____

6. Catherine은　그 얼룩을　빼내는 게 좋겠다 .

   _____

7. 우리는　그 해변에　가는 게 좋겠다 .

   _____

8. Jason은　코트를　입는 게 좋겠다 .

   _____

9. 너의 남동생은　자전거를　타지 않는 게 좋겠다 .

   _____

10. 너는　음식을　먹지 않는 게 좋겠다 .

    _____

다음의 우리말 표현을 영어로 쓰시오.

1 그의 누나는 <u>약간의</u> 약을 복용해야 한다.

His sister should take **some** medicine.

_____

2 그 <u>유명한</u> (famous) 선수는 달리기를 연습해야 한다.

_____

3 <u>모든</u> (all) 학생들은 그들의 숙제를 해야 한다.

_____

4 어린이들은 <u>많은</u> (many) 캐러멜들을 먹으면 안 된다.

_____

5 우리는 <u>시끄러운</u> (loud) 음악을 연주하면 안 된다.

_____

6 Catherine은 그 <u>검은</u> 얼룩을 빼내는 게 좋겠다.

_____

7 우리는 그 <u>아름다운</u> 해변에 가는 게 좋겠다.

_____

8 Jason은 <u>따뜻한</u> 코트를 입는 게 좋겠다.

_____

9 너의 <u>어린</u> (little) 남동생은 자전거를 타지 않는 게 좋겠다.

_____

10 너는 <u>매운</u> 음식을 먹지 않는 게 좋겠다.

_____

🐚 다음의 우리말 표현을 영어로 쓰시오.

1 그의 누나는 **고열때문에** 약간의 약을 복용해야 한다.

His sister should take some medicine **for a high fever** .

2 그 유명한 선수는 **마라톤 경기를 위해** (for the marathon) 달리기를 연습해야 한다.

_____

3 모든 학생들은 **방과 후에** (after school) 그들의 숙제를 해야 한다.

_____

4 어린이들은 **점심으로** (for their lunch) 많은 캐러멜들을 먹으면 안 된다.

_____

5 우리는 **밤에** (at night) 시끄러운 음악을 연주하면 안 된다.

_____

6 Catherine은 **표백제로** (with bleach) 그 검은 얼룩을 빼내는 게 좋겠다.

_____

7 우리는 **휴가로** (on vacation) 그 아름다운 해변에 가는 게 좋겠다.

_____

8 Jason은 **추운 날씨에** (in the cold weather) 따뜻한 코트를 입는 게 좋겠다.

_____

9 너의 어린 남동생은 **빙판길에서** (on the icy road) 자전거를 타지 않는 게 좋겠다.

_____

10 너는 **잠자리에 들기 전에** (before going to bed) 매운 음식을 먹지 않는 게 좋겠다.

_____

Unit 9 조동사 must, have to

☺ Writing에 필요한 문법

1. 조동사 must와 have to의 형태

must와 have(has) to 뒤에는 동사원형을 쓴다.

주어	조동사		동사원형
I	must	have to	return the books.
You / We / They			
He / She / It		has to	

2. 조동사 must가 있는 문장 맛보기

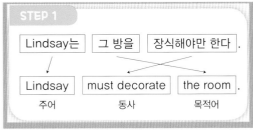

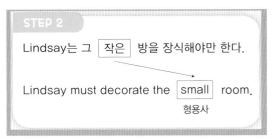

3. 조동사 must와 have to의 쓰임

쓰임	예문	해석
필요와 의무를 나타낼 때	We must listen to the teacher in class. We have to listen to the teacher in class.	-해야만 한다

* must는 '-임에 틀림없다'라는 뜻으로 강한 추측을 표현하기도 한다.
  The man must be rich.

4. 조동사 must와 have to의 기본 문장

종류	형태	예문
긍정문	주어+must/have(has) to+동사원형~.	They must clean their house today. They have to clean their house today.
부정문	주어+don't(doesn't) have to+동사원형~.	They don't have to clean their house today.
의문문	Do(Does)+주어+have to+동사원형~?	Do they have to clean their house today?

5. 조동사 must와 have to의 특징

must는 과거형이 없으므로 had to 사용	They musted go to shcool. (×) They had to go to school. (○)
must는 미래형이 없으므로 will have to 사용	They will must go to school. (×) They will have to go to school. (○)
have to의 부정은 don't have to를 사용하여 불필요를 표현(-할 필요가 없다)	You don't have to start the work right away.
must not(mustn't)은 강한 금지를 표현(-해서는 안된다)	You must not tell a lie.

🎙️ Writing에 필요한 문법 확인

A. 다음 중 알맞은 것을 고르시오.

1 You (must / mustn't) fasten your seatbelt in a car.

2 We (must / mustn't) be late for the meeting. It's very important.

3 Students (must / mustn't) use their cellphones in class.

4 I (must / mustn't) respect my parents.

B. have to를 이용하여 문장을 완성하시오.

1 Jack and Lisa have enough time. They _____ hurry up.

2 Kate wants to get a good grade. She _____ study hard.

3 Mark feels better now. He _____ take medicine anymore.

4 It will rain tomorrow. They _____ bring their umbrella.

C. 밑줄 친 부분을 must나 have to를 이용하여 바르게 고치시오.

1 They will <u>must write</u> a report for their homework.

2 Do we <u>has to cook</u> dinner tonight?

3 Don <u>musts feed</u> his dog every day.

4 Jane and Karen <u>musted meet</u> last week for their project.

5 He <u>doesn't has to go</u> to school today.

English	Korean	English	Korean
a lot of	많은	make money	돈을 벌다
buy	v. 사다	news	n. 소식, 뉴스
cute	adj. 예쁜, 귀여운	project	n. 프로젝트
decorate	v. 장식하다	send	v. 전하다, 보내다
delicious	adj. 맛있는	sick	adj. 아픈
dirty	adj. 더러운	urgent	adj. 급한
fix up	고치다, 수리하다	wash	v. 닦다

🐚 **다음의 우리말 표현을 영어로 쓰시오.**

1 Lindsay는 장식해야만 한다(must)   Lindsay must decorate

2 Jason은 닦아야만 한다(must)

3 나는 끝내야만 한다(have to)

4 그녀는 사야만 한다(have to)

5 그들은 수리할 필요가 없다

6 그는 -할 필요가 없다

7 너의 엄마는 만들어야만 한다(have to)

8 우리는 (돈을) 벌어야만 한다(have to)

9 Gary는 전해야만 했다

10 Cindy는 도와야만 할 것이다

🐚 **다음의 우리말 표현을 영어로 쓰시오.**

1. Lindsay는   그 방을   장식해야만 한다.
   Lindsay must decorate the room.
   주어   동사   목적어

2. Jason은   그의 차를   닦아야만 한다 .

   _____

3. 나는   그 프로젝트를   끝내야만 한다 .

   _____

4. 그녀는   인형을   사야만 한다 .

   _____

5. 그들은   그 집을   수리할 필요가 없다 .

   _____

6. 그는   그의 숙제를   할 필요가 없다 .

   _____

7. 너의 엄마는   케이크를   만드셔야만 하니 ?

   _____

8. 우리는   돈을   벌어야만 하니 ?

   _____

9. Gary는   그 소식을   전해야만 했다 .

   _____

10. Cindy는   사람들을   도와야만 할 것이다 .

    _____

🐚 **다음의 우리말 표현을 영어로 쓰시오.**

1 Lindsay는 그 작은 방을 장식해야만 한다.

   Lindsay must decorate the small room.

2 Jason은 그의 더러운 차를 닦아야만 한다.

_____

3 나는 그 새로운 프로젝트를 끝내야만 한다.

_____

4 그녀는 예쁜 인형을 사야만 한다.

_____

5 그들은 그 낡은 집을 수리할 필요가 없다.

_____

6 그는 그의 수학 숙제를 할 필요가 없다.

_____

7 너의 엄마는 맛있는 케이크를 만드셔야만 하니?

_____

8 우리는 많은 돈을 벌어야만 하니?

_____

9 Gary는 급한 소식을 전해야만 했다.

_____

10 Cindy는 아픈 사람들을 도와야만 할 것이다.

_____

🐚 **다음의 우리말 표현을 영어로 쓰시오.**

1 Lindsay는 그 작은 방을   다채로운 풍선으로   장식해야만 한다.

Lindsay must decorate the small room   with colorful balloons .

_____

2 Jason은 그의 더러운 차를   일요일에 (on Sunday) 닦아야만 한다.

_____

3 나는 그 새로운 프로젝트를   다음 달까지 (by next month) 끝내야만 한다.

_____

4 그녀는   여동생의 생일선물로 (for her sister's birthday) 예쁜 인형을 사야만 한다.

_____

5 그들은 그 낡은 집을   다음 주까지 (by next week) 수리할 필요가 없다.

_____

6 그는   주말에 (on the weekend) 그의 수학 숙제를 할 필요가 없다.

_____

7 너의 엄마는   파티를 위해 (for the party) 맛있는 케이크를 만드셔야만 하니?

_____

8 우리는   더 나은 삶을 위해 (for a better life) 많은 돈을 벌어야만 하니?

_____

9 Gary는   그의 친구에게 (to his friend) 급한 소식을 전해야만 했다.

_____

10 Cindy는   병원에서 (in the hospital) 아픈 사람들을 도와야만 할 것이다.

_____

More Practice

A. 주어진 단어를 사용하여 문장을 완성하시오.

1 we / before the end of April / have to / make cakes / for the school party / .

_____

2 during the hot day / had better not / you / in the park / ride a bicycle / .

_____

3 cannot / you / during the performance / use a mobile phone / .

_____

4 can / you / take some flowers / for your mom's birthday gift / from my garden / .

_____

B. 다음 문장을 영작하시오.

1 너는 감기가 낫기 위해서 이 약을 아침 식사 후와 저녁 식사 후 두 번 다 복용해야만 한다. (must, to get over your cold)

_____

2 인도에서 온 이 코끼리는 몇 가지 한국말 단어를 이해할 수 있다. (from India, can, some Korean words)

_____

3 너는 밤에 소란을 피우면 안 된다. (should, make a noise)

_____

4 너는 너의 새 스웨터를 세탁기에 넣어서 빨면 안 된다. (should, in a washing machine)

_____

🐚 다음 표를 보고 각 인물들이 할 수 있는 것과 할수 없는 것을 문장으로 묘사하시오.

	can	cannot
David		
Justin		
Kelly		
Sophia		
Brian		

1 David can swim but he can't _____.

2 Justin _____ but _____.

3 Kelly _____ but _____.

4 Sophia _____ but _____.

5 Brian _____ but _____.

to부정사 1 (명사 역할)

 Writing에 필요한 문법

1. to부정사의 형태

기본형태	to+동사원형	To read books is interesting.
부정형	not to+동사원형	His hope is not to do homework.

2. to부정사 문장 맛보기

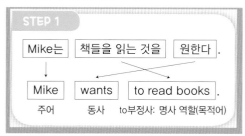

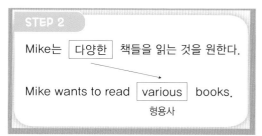

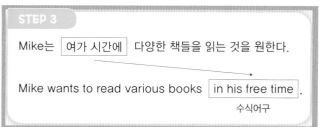

3. to부정사의 쓰임

쓰임		예문	해석
명사 역할	주어	To read good books is important. = It is important to read good books. (가주어)　　　　　(진주어) * 주어로 쓰일 때에는 항상 단수 동사를 취한다.	-하는 것
	목적어	Jason loves to read good books. * to 부정사를 목적어로 취하는 동사 　like, love, begin, start, ask, decide, expect, hope, wish, 　learn, need, plan, promise, want, agree, choose 등	
	보어	His hobby is to read books.	

Writing에 필요한 문법 확인

A. 다음 중 알맞은 것을 고르시오.

1 It is not easy (understand / to understand) teenage girls.

2 My dream is (travel / to travel) around the world.

3 (Learn / To learn) foreign languages is necessary.

4 It is useful (carry / to carry) some coins.

5 Every boy knows how (play / to play) basketball.

B. 주어진 문장을 가주어 it을 사용하여 다시 쓰시오.

1 To study math is difficult.

→ _____

2 To swim in this pool makes me feel good.

→ _____

3 To visit foreign countries is a lot of fun.

→ _____

4 To exercise regularly is necessary.

→ _____

5 To go to a concert is exciting.

→ _____

C. 주어진 동사를 이용하여 문장을 완성하시오.

1 It is hard _____ a high mountain such as Mount Everest. (climb)
(에베레스트 산 같은 높은 산을 등산하는 것은 어렵다.)

2 It is important _____ healthy food. (eat)
(건강한 음식을 먹는 것은 중요하다.)

3 It is dangerous _____ under the hot sun. (swim)
(뜨거운 태양 아래서 수영하는 것은 위험하다.)

4 They expected _____ the nice house by the river. (buy)
(그들은 강가에 있는 좋은 집을 사는 것을 기대했다.)

5 David's plan is _____ his cousins at the family reunion. (meet)
(David의 계획은 가족 모임에서 사촌들을 만나는 것이다.)

English	Korean	English	Korean
childhood	n. 어린 시절	New Year's resolution	새해 결심
cure	n. 치유법	raw	adj. 익히지 않은
develop	v. 개발하다	safe	adj. 안전한
have a snowball fight	눈싸움을 하다	set a goal	목표를 정하다
keep a secret	비밀을 지키다	shelter	n. 보호소
look after	돌보다	step	n. 단계
master	v. 완전히 배우다	vegetable	n. 채소

🐚 다음의 우리말 표현을 영어로 쓰시오.

1 책들을 읽는 것

   to read books

2 TV 프로그램을 보는 것(watch a TV program)

3 눈 싸움을 하는 것

4 치유법을 개발하는 것

5 그 작문 수업을 듣지 않는 것(take the writing course)

6 채소들을 먹는 것

7 그 비밀을 지키는 것

8 그 동물들을 돌보는 것

9 너의 목표를 정하는 것

10 외국어들을 완전히 배우는 것(foreign languages)

🐚 **다음의 우리말 표현을 영어로 쓰시오.**

1 Mike는 책들을 읽는 것을 원한다.

  Mike wants to read books.
  주어   동사   목적어

2 TV 프로그램을 보는 것은 도움이 (helpful) 된다 .

_____

3 눈싸움을 하는 것은 재미 (fun) 있다 .

_____

4 그는 치유법을 개발하는 것을 원했다 .

_____

5 그는 그 작문 수업을 듣지 않기로 결심했다 (decide).

_____

6 그들은 채소들을 먹는 것을 시작했다 (start).

_____

7 그들은 그 비밀을 지킬 것을 약속했다 (promise).

_____

8 그의 일은 (his job) 그 동물들을 돌보는 것 이다 .

_____

9 첫 번째 단계는 (the first step) 너의 목표를 정하는 것 이다 .

_____

10 그의 새해 결심은 외국어들을 완전히 배우는 것 이다 .

_____

🐚 **다음의 우리말 표현을 영어로 쓰시오.**

1 Mike는 [다양한] 책들을 읽는 것을 원한다.

   Mike wants to read various books.

2 [좋은] (good) TV 프로그램을 보는 것은 도움이 된다.

3 [친구들과] 눈싸움을 하는 것은 재미있다.

4 그는 [그 질병의] (for the disease) 치유법을 개발하는 것을 원했다.

5 그는 [3주] (three-week) 작문 수업을 듣지 않기로 결심했다.

6 그들은 [익히지 않은] 채소들을 먹는 것을 시작했다.

7 그들은 [중대한] (big) 비밀을 지킬 것을 약속했다.

8 그의 일은 [야생의] (wild) 동물들을 돌보는 것이다.

9 첫 번째 단계는 너의 목표를 [명확하게] (clearly) 정하는 것이다.

10 그의 새해 결심은 [다섯 개의] 외국어들을 완전히 배우는 것이다.

🐚 다음의 우리말 표현을 영어로 쓰시오.

1   Mike는   여가 시간에   다양한 책들을 읽는 것을 원한다.

     Mike wants to read various books   in his free time .
_____

2   좋은 TV 프로그램을 보는 것은   아이들의 교육을 위해 (for children's education) 도움이 된다.
_____

3   친구들과   방과 후에 (after school) 눈싸움을 하는 것은 재미있다.
_____

4   그는   그 해 말까지 (by the end of the year) 그 질병의 치유법을 개발하는 것을 원했다.
_____

5   그는   여름에 (for the summer) 3주 작문 수업을 듣지 않기로 결심했다.
_____

6   그들은   더 나은 건강을 위해 (for better health) 익히지 않은 채소들을 먹는 것을 시작했다.
_____

7   그들은   지속적인 우정을 위해 (for a lasting friendship) 중대한 비밀을 지킬 것을 약속했다.
_____

8   그의 일은   그 보호소에 있는   야생의 동물들을 돌보는 것이다.
_____

9   첫 번째 단계는   미래를 위해 (for the future) 너의 목표를 명확하게 정하는 것이다.
_____

10   그의 새해 결심은   세계 여행을 위해서 (for world travel) 다섯 개의 외국어들을 완전히 배우는 것이다.
_____

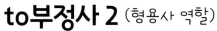

to부정사 2 (형용사 역할)

Writing에 필요한 문법

1. 형용사로 쓰이는 to부정사의 형태

기본 형태	명사+to+동사원형	David has many books to read. I built a house to live in.

2. to부정사 문장 맛보기

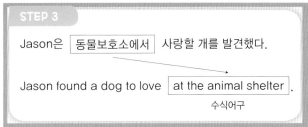

3. to부정사의 쓰임

쓰임	예문	해석
명사 뒤에서 명사를 수식하는 형용사 역할	Sarah has many skirts to wear. Do you want something to eat?	-(해야) 할, -하는

Writing에 필요한 문법 확인

A. 밑줄 친 to부정사의 쓰임에 체크(V)하시오.

		명사	형용사
1	It is fun <u>to play</u> basketball.	☐	☐
2	My grandma found a chair <u>to sit</u> on.	☐	☐
3	David wants <u>to be</u> a great writer.	☐	☐
4	Please give this boy something <u>to eat</u>.	☐	☐
5	Sarah needs a friend <u>to play</u> with.	☐	☐

B. 주어진 동사를 이용하여 문장을 완성하시오.

1 There are many things _____ from David. (learn)
　(David로부터 배울 많은 것들이 있다.)

2 Kate has many winter coats _____ . (wear)
　(Kate는 입을 많은 겨울코트를 가지고 있다.)

3 The students borrowed a pen _____ . (write with)
　(그 학생들은 쓸 펜을 빌렸다.)

4 James had math homework _____ yesterday. (do)
　(James는 어제 해야 할 수학 숙제가 있었다.)

5 I need a smart person _____ my computer. (fix)
　(나는 내 컴퓨터를 고쳐 줄 똑똑한 사람이 필요하다.)

C. 주어진 단어를 사용하여 문장을 완성하시오.

1 He has _____ him. (no / help / to / friends)

2 She is a pleasant _____ . (to / person / talk to)

3 David wants some _____ . (read / books / to)

4 She needs some _____ . (to / paper / write on)

5 Every student has _____ . (wear / a school uniform / to)

English	Korean	English	Korean
carry	v. 운반하다	live in	-에 거주하다
colored pencil	색연필	moving day	이사 날
draw with	-로 그리다	own	v. 소유하다
during a lunch break	점심 시간 동안	play soccer with	-와 축구 하다
emergency	n. 비상(상황)	solve	v. 해결하다
first	adj. 최초의	spend on	(돈 등을) -에 쓰다
inexpensive	adj. 비싸지 않은	wash	v. 닦다

다음의 우리말 표현을 영어로 쓰시오.

1 사랑할 개

a dog to love

2 방문한 최초의 한국인

3 축구를 함께 할 친구들

4 닦아야 할 접시들(dishes)

5 거주할 집

6 그림을 그릴 색연필들

7 해결해야 할 문제들

8 운반해야 할 상자들

9 마실 차가운 무언가

10 쓸 돈

🐚 다음의 우리말 표현을 영어로 쓰시오.

1 Jason은   개를   발견했다.
   ↓
   Jason   found   a dog.
   주어   동사   목적어

2 그는   최초의 한국인   이었다 .

   _____

3 나는   친구들을   원한다 .

   _____

4 접시들이   있었다 (there were).

   _____

5 그들은   집을   소유하고 있었다 .

   _____

6 Mike는   색연필들을 사기를   원한다 .

   _____

7 우리는   문제들을   가지고 있었다 .

   _____

8 Kate는   상자들을   가지고 있었다 .

   _____

9 David는   차가운 무언가를   원한다 .

   _____

10 그 형제들은 (the brothers)   돈을   가지고 있었다 .

   _____

🐚 **다음의 우리말 표현을 영어로 쓰시오.**

1 Jason은 ｜사랑할｜ 개를 발견했다.

Jason found a dog to love .

2 그는 ｜미국을 방문한｜ 최초의 한국인이었다.

_____

3 나는 ｜축구를 함께 할｜ 친구들을 원한다.

_____

4 ｜닦아야 할｜ 접시들이 있었다.

_____

5 그들은 ｜거주할｜ 집을 소유하고 있었다.

_____

6 Mike는 ｜그림을 그릴｜ 색연필들을 사기를 원한다.

_____

7 우리는 ｜해결해야 할｜ 문제들을 가지고 있었다.

_____

8 Kate는 ｜운반해야 할｜ 상자들을 가지고 있었다.

_____

9 David는 ｜마실｜ 차가운 무언가를 원한다.

_____

10 그 형제들은 ｜쓸｜ 돈을 가지고 있었다.

_____

🐚 **다음의 우리말 표현을 영어로 쓰시오.**

1 Jason은 동물보호소에서 사랑할 개를 발견했다.

   Jason found a dog to love at the animal shelter .

   _____

2 그는 조선시대에 (in the Joseon Dynasty) 미국을 방문한 최초의 한국인이었다.

   _____

3 나는 점심 시간 동안 축구를 함께 할 친구들을 원한다.

   _____

4 파티가 끝난 후 (after the party) 닦아야 할 접시들이 있었다.

   _____

5 그들은 그 당시에 (at the time) 거주할 집을 소유하고 있었다.

   _____

6 Mike는 그림을 그릴 비싸지 않은 색연필들을 사기를 원한다.

   _____

7 우리는 위급 상황에 (during the emergency) 해결해야 할 문제들을 가지고 있었다.

   _____

8 Kate는 이사 날에 (on her moving day) 운반해야 할 상자들을 가지고 있었다.

   _____

9 David는 운동 후에 (after exercise) 마실 차가운 무언가를 원한다.

   _____

10 그 형제들은 엄마의 생일 선물에 (on their mom's birthday present) 쓸 돈을 가지고
   있었다.

   _____

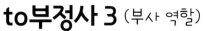

to부정사 3 (부사 역할)

 Writing에 필요한 문법

1. 부사로 쓰이는 to부정사의 형태

기본형태	예문
(in order) to+동사원형 * in order는 주로 생략	Mike visited the school library to study.
형용사+to+동사원형	I'm so happy to see you. This math problem is difficult to solve fast.

2. to부정사 문장 맛보기

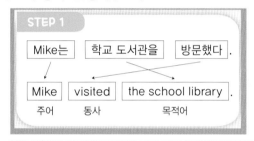

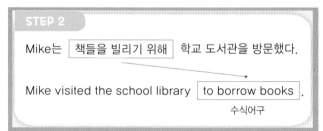

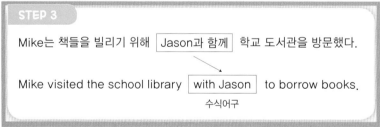

3. to부정사의 쓰임

쓰임	예문	해석
목적	She went to the market to buy some food.	-하기 위해서
형용사 수식	This book is difficult to read.	-하기에
감정의 원인	I'm so happy to tell you this good news.	-하게 되어
판단의 근거	You are brave to help the people in the fire.	-하는 것을 보니

4. to 부정사의 관용 표현

형태	예문	해석
too+형용사+to+동사원형	I was too tired to clean the room.	너무 -해서 -할 수 없다
enough+명사+to+동사원형	Brian has enough talent to become an actor.	-할 만큼 충분한
형용사+enough+to+동사원형	Jenny is old enough to drive a car.	-할 만큼 충분히 -하다

Writing에 필요한 문법 확인

A. 밑줄 친 to부정사를 해석하시오.

1 Steve started to save money to buy a new computer. _____

2 David is too young to travel alone. _____

3 He is rich enough to buy the expensive car. _____

4 The robbers made a plan to steal money. _____

5 I'm so sorry to hear the bad news. _____

B. 주어진 단어를 사용하여 문장을 완성하시오.

1 The food in this restaurant is _____. (make / difficult / to)

2 David is _____ our study team. (enough / to / smart / join)

3 Jason was _____ the room. (to / tired / clean / too)

4 Tom didn't have _____ milk for his cat. (money / enough / buy / to)

5 I ran _____ the bus. (enough / catch / fast / to)

C. 주어진 단어를 사용하여 문장을 완성하시오.

1 is / to sit on / this chair / not / comfortable / .

_____

2 he / clever / be / to solve the quiz / must / .

_____

3 strong / to win the game / were / enough / they / .

_____

4 go to the park / after dinner / to take a walk / they / .

_____

5 baked a cake / Jen / to celebrate / her mom's birthday / .

_____

English	Korean	English	Korean
architecture	n. 건축물	maintain health	건강을 유지하다
castle	n. 성	master	v. 완전히 습득하다
cross	v. 건너다	recommend	v. 추천하다
donate	v. 기부하다	refrigerator	n. 냉장고
exhibition	n. 전시회	regular exercise	규칙적인 운동
forest	n. 숲	savings	n. 예금
in a short time	단시간 안에	survive	v. (위기 등을) 견뎌내다

다음의 우리말 표현을 영어로 쓰시오.

1 책들을 빌리기 위해   to borrow books

2 그 버스를 잡기 위해(catch)

3 그의 건축물을 보기 위해

4 건강을 유지하기 위해서

5 가난한 아이들을 돕기 위해서(poor)

6 스페인어를 배우기 위해(Spanish)

7 완전히 습득하기에 너무 어려운

8 지진을 견뎌내기 위해서(an earthquake)

9 그 냉장고를 옮길 정도로 충분히(move)

10 그 다리를 건너기에는 너무 무거운(bridge)

🐚 **다음의 우리말 표현을 영어로 쓰시오.**

1. Mike는　학교 도서관을　방문했다.

   Mike　visited　the school library.
   주어　　동사　　목적어

2. David는　빠르게　뛰었다 .

   _____

3. Jason은　Gaudi 전시회에　갔다 .

   _____

4. 규칙적인 운동은　추천된다 .

   _____

5. 그는　그의 예금 중 일부를 (some of his savings)　기부할 것이다 .

   _____

6. Kevin은　그 수업을 듣기로 (take the class)　결심했다 .

   _____

7. 이 언어는　너무　어렵다 .

   _____

8. 이 성은　건축되었다 (build).

   _____

9. Mike는　충분히　힘이 세다 .

   _____

10. 그 코끼리는　너무　무거웠다 .

    _____

🐚 **다음의 우리말 표현을 영어로 쓰시오.**

1 Mike는 책들을 빌리기 위해 학교 도서관을 방문했다.

   Mike visited the school library to borrow books .

2 David는 그 버스를 잡기 위해 빠르게 뛰었다.

   _____

3 Jason은 Gaudi 전시회에 그의 건축물을 보기 위해 갔다.

   _____

4 규칙적인 운동은 건강을 유지하기 위해서 추천된다.

   _____

5 그는 그의 예금 중 일부를 가난한 아이들을 돕기 위해서 기부할 것이다.

   _____

6 Kevin은 스페인어를 배우기 위해 그 수업을 듣기로 결심했다.

   _____

7 이 언어는 완전히 습득하기에 너무 어렵다.

   _____

8 이 성은 지진을 견뎌내기 위해서 건축되었다.

   _____

9 Mike는 무거운 냉장고를 옮길 정도로 (move the heavy refrigerator) 충분히 힘이 세다.

   _____

10 그 코끼리는 그 나무 다리를 건너기에는 (cross the wooden bridge) 너무 무거웠다.

   _____

🐚 다음의 우리말 표현을 영어로 쓰시오.

1 Mike는 책들을 빌리기 위해   Jason과 함께   학교 도서관을 방문했다.

Mike visited the school library with Jason   to borrow books.

---

2 David는   뉴욕에 가는 (to New York) 버스를 잡기 위해 빠르게 뛰었다.

---

3 Jason은   주말에 (on the weekend) Gaudi 전시회에 그의 건축물을 보기 위해 갔다.

---

4 규칙적인 운동은   좋은   건강을 유지하기 위해서 추천된다.

---

5 그는   조만간 (in the near future) 그의 예금 중 일부를 가난한 아이들을 돕기 위해서 기부할 것이다.

---

6 Kevin은   스페인 8주 방문 후 (after his eight-week visit of Spain) 스페인어를 배우기 위해 그 수업을 듣기로 결심했다.

---

7 이 언어는   단시간 안에   완전히 습득하기에 너무 어렵다.

---

8 이 성은 지진을 견뎌내기 위해서   고대 이집트인들에 의해 (by ancient Egyptians) 건축되었다.

---

9 Mike는 무거운 냉장고를   두 번 (twice) 옮길 정도로 충분히 힘이 세다.

---

10 그 코끼리는   숲에 있는 (in the forest) 나무 다리를 건너기에는 너무 무거웠다.

More Practice

A. 주어진 단어를 사용하여 문장을 완성하시오.

1　to buy a new car / money / should / Mike / save / .

_____

2　went to the library / Sarah / to borrow some books / near her school / .

_____

3　to solve the math problems / without a calculator / it is impossible / in 30 minutes / .

_____

4　ran / we / to catch the last bus / fast / at night / .

_____

B. 다음 문장을 영작하시오.

1　James는 약간의 음식을 사기 위해 집 근처의 슈퍼마켓을 갔다. (near his house)

_____

2　나는 시험에서 좋은 점수를 얻기 위해 많은 시간을 공부했다. (get a good score on the test)

_____

3　올해 나의 계획은 학교에 정각에 도착하기 위해서 아침에 일찍 일어나는 것이다. (get up early in the morning to be on time)

_____

4　너는 이 도서관의 규칙들을 지키기 위해서 목소리를 낮춰야 한다. (must keep down your voice)

_____

Creative Thinking Activity

🐚 다음 표를 보고 to부정사를 사용하여 문장을 완성하시오.

	want	doesn't want
Mom	clean the house	go swimming go to a movie
Justin	go to the movie go swimming	clean the house go shopping
Brian	go to a museum go swimming	clean the house go to a movie

Mom: Hi Justin and Brian. What do you want to do today?

Justin: Sally said the new animation "Cars" is good. I want _____ _____ .

Brian: I already saw it with Alice. I want _____ or _____ . What do you want to do with us, Mom?

Mom: Going to a museum sounds great, but I want _____ .

Brian: Oh no, Mom. Today is the hottest day. I don't want to do any work.

Justin: Brian is right. I don't want _____ on this hot day. How about going swimming?

Mom: All right, boys. I don't want _____ , but I am going to go with you.

등위접속사 1

[Writing에 필요한 문법 확인]   p.7

A. 1 or   2 and   3 but   4 and   5 but

B. 1 David got a toy car∨ a book(∨) and a ball for his birthday.

   2 I read two or three books every month. X

   3 Which color do you like, yellow, green(∨) or blue? X

   4 The baker needs some sugar∨ salt, and flour to make cookies.

   5 He was poor but happy. X

C. 1 Kevin loves his mom and dad.

   2 The problem looks difficult but is simple.

   3 Would you like some bread or rice?

   4 I need a pencil, a notebook, and an eraser.

   5 I will buy a scarf, a bag, or a hat.

[Warm Up : 표현 만들기]   p.8

2 a Spanish class and a Chinese class

3 vegetables, fruits, and flowers

4 pasta, rice, or steak

5 swimming and fishing

6 in the morning and in the evening

7 this week or next week

8 nice but expensive

9 old but fast

10 smile but not happy

[Step 1 : 문장 시작하기]   p.9

2 Did you take a Spanish class?

3 Do you grow vegetables?

4 I will cook pasta.

5 They enjoyed swimming.

6 He works out in the morning.

7 She will leave this week.

8 The shoes are nice.

9 My computer is old.

10 The singer smiles.

[Step 2 : 문장 완성하기]   p.10

2 Did you take a Spanish class and a Chinese class ?

3 Do you grow vegetables, fruits, and flowers ?

4 I will cook pasta, rice, or steak .

5 They enjoyed swimming and fishing .

6 He works out in the morning and in the evening .

7 She will leave this week or next week .

8 The shoes are nice but expensive .

9 My computer is old but fast .

10 The singer smiles but he is not happy .

[Step 3 : 문장 꾸미기]   p.11

2 Did you take a Spanish class and a Chinese class last year ?

3 Do you grow vegetables, fruits, and flowers in the garden ?

4 I will cook pasta, rice, or steak for my friends .

5 They enjoyed swimming and fishing in the sea .

6 He works out in the morning and in the evening for his health .

7 She will leave for Canada this week or next week.

8 The shoes in the store are nice but expensive.

9 My computer on the desk is old but fast.

10 The singer on stage smiles but he is not happy.

상관접속사 2

[Writing에 필요한 문법 확인]   p.13

A. 1 nor   2 but   3 and   4 or   5 but also

B. 1 reading, writing

   2 a poet, a novelist

   3 his phone number, his address

C. 1 Both, and　　　2 either, or

3 not only, but also　　4 not, but

5 both, and

[Warm Up : 표현 만들기]　　　p.14

2 either dance or sing

3 both food and medicine

4 neither ate food nor made friends

5 like not milk but juice

6 not Sarah's husband but her son

7 either during summer vacation or during winter vacation

8 not only hot but also humid

9 not only played but also composed

10 neither laugh nor cry

[Step 1 : 문장 시작하기]　　　p.15

2 Mike will dance.

3 People need food.

4 Greg ate food.

5 She likes milk.

6 Sarah's husband bought some roses.

7 David visited his grandmother during summer vacation.

8 The days are too hot.

9 Mozart played the piano.

10 The actress laughs.

[Step 2 : 문장 완성하기]　　　p.16

2 Mike will either dance or sing .

3 People need both food and medicine .

4 Greg neither ate food nor made friends .

5 She likes not milk but juice .

6 Not Sarah's husband but her son bought some roses.

7 David visited his grandmother either during summer vacation or during winter vacation .

8 The days are not only too hot but also too humid .

9 Mozart not only played the piano but also composed music .

10 The actress neither laughs nor cries .

[Step 3 : 문장 꾸미기]　　　p.17

2 Mike will either dance or sing for a(the) school talent show .

3 People need both food and medicine for survival .

4 Greg neither ate food nor made friends at the party .

5 She likes not milk but juice on her breakfast cereal .

6 Not Sarah's husband but her son bought some roses for her birthday gift .

7 David visited his grandmother in London either during summer vacation or during winter vacation.

8 The days are not only too hot but also too humid for taking a walk .

9 Mozart not only played the piano but also composed music at a very early age .

10 The actress neither laughs nor cries in the movie .

3 현재완료 1 (계속, 완료)

[Writing에 필요한 문법 확인]　　　p.19-20

A. 1 went　　　2 has taught　　3 studied

4 has learned　　5 have known

B. 1 moved　　2 has, eaten　　3 have prepared

4 rained　　5 haven't read

[Warm Up : 표현 만들기]　　　p.20

2 People have written

3 Volunteers have provided

4 Scientists have warned

5 He has worked on

6 They have lived

7 Mike has built

8 Firefighters have saved

9 They have collected

10 Jason has met

[Step 1 : 문장 시작하기]   p.21

2 People have written books.

3 Volunteers have provided food.

4 Scientists have warned us.

5 He has worked on the statue.

6 They have lived in a city.

7 Mike has built a website.

8 Firefighters have saved lives.

9 They have collected books.

10 Jason has met people.

[Step 2 : 문장 완성하기]   p.22

2 People have written books about the serious problems .

3 Volunteers have provided food to the homeless .

4 Scientists have warned us about air pollution .

5 He has worked on the huge statue.

6 They have lived in a big city.

7 Mike has built a large-scale website.

8 Firefighters have saved valuable lives.

9 They have collected rare books.

10 Jason has met various people.

[Step 3 : 문장 꾸미기]   p.23

2 People have written books about the serious problems of poverty .

3 Volunteers have provided food to the homeless for three years .

4 Scientists have warned us about air pollution several times .

5 He has worked on the huge statue for ten years .

6 They have lived in a big city since last year .

7 Mike has built a large-scale website without

any difficulties .

8 Firefighters have saved valuable lives in spite of many difficulties .

9 They have collected rare books for seven years .

10 Jason has met various people since the summer of 2015 .

Check Up 1. Unit 1-3

[More Practice]   p.24

A. 1 Both Paris and London are Sally's favorite cities in Europe.

2 Peter was neither at school nor at home last Monday.

3 David not only plays the piano but also plays the flute well.

4 Sam has swum for one hour at the pool. / Sam has swum at the pool for one hour.

B. 1 David has watered the plants in his grandmother's garden since last year.

2 Not only Jake but also Greg bought a new toy in the big toy store.

3 Drake has written over twenty books about the history of England.

4 James has already finished two writing courses(classes) with success.

[Creative Thinking Activity]   p.25

2 Justin has studied drawing at NY Art School since 2010.

3 Ken has taught Italian since 2011.

4 James has created advertisements for Pear Company since 2012.

5 Jack has written novels for children since 2013.

4 현재완료 2 (경험, 결과)

[Writing에 필요한 문법 확인]   p.27

A. 1 seen → have seen   2 Have → Has

3 never read → have never read

4 see → seen　　　5 invite → invited

B. 1 Have, met　　　2 Has, had

3 has never lived　　4 have talked

5 has used

C. 1 Have, seen　　　2 has never finished

3 have worked　　4 has, been to

5 has, taken

[Warm Up : 표현 만들기]　　　p.28

2 The children haven't seen

3 Jacob has painted

4 The Korean team has reached

5 Mike has repaired

6 The boy has broken

7 Ken has washed

8 I have learned

9 Brian has made

10 Peter has written

[Step 1 : 문장 시작하기]　　　p.29

2 The children haven't seen snow.

3 Jacob has painted his bedroom.

4 The Korean team has reached the semifinals.

5 Mike has repaired cars.

6 The boy has broken his leg.

7 Ken has washed his sneakers.

8 I have learned football.

9 Brian has made food.

10 Peter has written short stories.

[Step 2 : 문장 완성하기]　　　p.30

2 The children have never seen snow.

3 Jacob has painted his bedroom blue .

4 The Korean team has reached the semifinals
of the World Cup .

5 Mike has repaired broken cars.

6 The boy has broken his leg three times .

7 Ken has washed his sneakers by hand .

8 I have learned football from David .

9 Brian has made special food.

10 Peter has written short stories for young
children .

[Step 3 : 문장 꾸미기]　　　p.31

2 The children in Africa have never seen snow.

3 Jacob has painted his bedroom blue three
times .

4 The Korean team has reached the semifinals
of the World Cup once .

5 Mike has repaired broken cars several times .

6 The active boy has broken his leg three
times.

7 Ken has washed his sneakers by hand twice .

8 I have learned football from David in
America .

9 Brian has made special food for his sick
mother .

10 Peter has written short stories for young
children before .

🌩 5 지각동사

[Writing에 필요한 문법 확인]　　　p.33-34

A. 1 good　2 interesting　3 go　4 tap

5 come

B. 1 ⓒ　2 ⓒ　3 ⓓ　4 ⓓ　5 ⓓ

C. 1 He heard my dogs bark.

2 The muffin smells good.

3 I heard you talk on the phone.

[Warm Up : 표현 만들기]　　　p.34

2 looked at the sun　　3 heard my cats

4 listened to their teacher　5 felt her dog

6 heard water　　　7 felt some bug

8 saw his dad

9 smelled something

10 watched some pandas

[Step 1 : 문장 시작하기]   p.35

2 She looked at the sun rising.

3 I heard my cats meow.

4 They listened to their teacher talk about the final exam.

5 She felt her dog coming to her.

6 Mom heard water boiling.

7 I felt some bug crawl on my body.

8 He saw his dad wash the dishes.

9 I smelled something cooking.

10 The boy watched some pandas eat bamboo.

[Step 2 : 문장 완성하기]   p.36

2 She looked at the sun rising from the horizon.

3 I heard my cats meow loudly.

4 They carefully listened to their teacher talk about the final exam.

5 She felt her dog coming closer to her.

6 Mom heard water boiling in the pot.

7 I felt some bug crawl on my body in the forest.

8 He saw his dad wash the dishes after a snack.

9 I smelled something cooking in the kitchen.

10 The boy watched some pandas eat a lot of bamboo.

[Step 3 : 문장 꾸미기]   p.37

2 She looked at the sun rising from the horizon above the mountain.

3 I heard my cats meow loudly in the bedroom.

4 They carefully listened to their teacher talk about the final exam in class.

5 She felt her dog coming closer to her on the bed.

6 Mom heard water boiling in the pot on the kitchen counter.

7 I felt some bug crawl on my body in the forest a few minutes ago.

8 He saw his dad wash the dishes after a snack

last night.

9 I smelled something cooking in the kitchen from my neighbor's house.

10 The boy watched some pandas eat a lot of bamboo at the zoo.

🌩 6 수동태

[Writing에 필요한 문법 확인]   p.39-40

A. 1 is written   2 was painted   3 was taught
   4 eat   5 will hold

B. 1 is repaired   2 was painted
   3 will be moved   4 were eaten
   5 by a mosquito

C. 1 A computer is being fixed by my brother.
   2 The window was broken by me yesterday.
   3 The thief was caught by the police.
   4 The comic book is read by them.
   5 The computer game was played by Susan and her sister.

[Warm Up : 표현 만들기]   p.40

2 The story wasn't written

3 A house will be built

4 I was invited

5 The work will not be finished

6 The theory is being explained

7 The radio is turned on

8 The food is served

9 Languages are taught

10 The idea was suggested

[Step 1 : 문장 시작하기]   p.41

2 The story wasn't written by Jay.

3 A house will be built by my father.

4 I was invited by my friend.

5 The work will not be finished by them.

6 The theory is being explained by my professor.

7 The radio is turned on by me.

8 The food is served by the waiter.

9 Languages are taught by teachers.

10 The idea was suggested by my parents.

[Step 2 : 문장 완성하기]   p.42

2 The sad story wasn't written by Jay.

3 A big house will be built by my father.

4 I was invited by my best friend.

5 The hard work will not be finished by them.

6 The new theory is being explained by my professor.

7 The red radio is turned on by me.

8 The food is served by the tall waiter.

9 Foreign languages are taught by teachers.

10 The good idea was suggested by my parents.

[Step 3 : 문장 꾸미기]   p.43

2 The sad story wasn't written by Jay in 2010.

3 A big house will be built by my father next year.

4 I was invited to the wedding by my best friend.

5 The hard work will not be finished by them on time.

6 The new theory is being explained by my professor at the seminar.

7 The red radio is turned on by me every night.

8 The food is served by the tall waiter at the restaurant.

9 Foreign languages are taught by teachers at school.

10 The good idea was suggested by my parents last month.

Check Up 2. Unit 4-6

[More Practice]   p.44

A. 1 The floor is covered with sand and water after the storm.

2 A snowmobile was made by two men to travel on snow and ice.

3 Mike has asked his parents for help three times.

4 We felt the house shaking for two minutes yesterday.

B. 1 I haven't eaten both Chinese and Thai food at a restaurant before.

2 This smart dog from London has won the award in a world dog competition twice.

3 The famous play *Romeo and Juliet* was not written by J. K. Rowling but by William Shakespeare.

4 I saw the smart dog help his family in many ways.

[Creative Thinking Activity]   p.45

1 The *Harry Potter* series was written by J. K. Rowling.

2 The Eiffel Tower was built by Gustave Eiffel.

3 The film *Modern Times* was made by Charlie Chaplin.

4 *The Weeping Woman* was painted by Pablo Picasso.

5 The opera Don *Giovanni* was composed by Amadeus Mozart.

Unit 7 조동사 can, may

[Writing에 필요한 문법 확인]   p.47-48

A. 1 fails → fail

2 can't → couldn't

3 can drove → can drive

4 couldn't saw → couldn't see

5 speaks → speak

B. 1 may go hiking   2 May (Can), ask

3 can't take pictures   4 couldn't save

5 can't play soccer

[Warm Up : 표현 만들기]   p.48

2 He can graduate   3 She may not finish

4 They could not provide

5 A snake can kill   6 Cooper could prove

7 Her son could play

8 Students may complain

9 He may overcome   10 I could save

[Step 1 : 문장 시작하기]   p.49

2 He can graduate from university.

3 She may not finish the history project.

4 They could not provide food.

5 A snake can kill you.

6 Cooper could prove the cause of the accident.

7 Her son could play the violin.

8 Students may complain of stomachaches.

9 He may overcome the difficulty.

10 I could save money.

[Step 2 : 문장 완성하기]   p.50

2 He can graduate from university this year.

3 She may not finish the challenging history project.

4 They could not provide enough food.

5 A poisonous snake can kill you.

6 Cooper could prove the cause of the accident clearly.

7 Her talented son could play the violin.

8 Students in this school may complain of stomachaches.

9 He may completely overcome the difficulty.

10 I could save a lot of money.

[Step 3 : 문장 꾸미기]   p.51

2 He can finally graduate from university this year.

3 She may not finish the challenging history project on time.

4 They could not provide enough food to the

homeless.

5 A poisonous snake can kill you in an instant.

6 Thanks to government, Cooper could prove the cause of the accident clearly.

7 Her talented son could play the violin at the age of two.

8 Because of spoiled milk, students in this school may complain of stomachaches.

9 He may completely overcome the difficulty with a positive attitude.

10 I could save a lot of money without help from my parents.

Unit 8 조동사 should, had better

[Writing에 필요한 문법 확인]   p.53-54

A. 1 should protect   2 should follow

3 shouldn't cross   4 should eat

5 shouldn't play

B. 1 had better   2 had better not

3 had better   4 had better

5 had better not

C. 1 shoulds → should   2 You'ad → You'd

3 cleaned → clean   4 studying → study

5 doesn't → not

[Warm Up : 표현 만들기]   p.54

2 should practice

3 should do one's homework

4 should not eat   5 should not play

6 had better take out   7 had better go

8 had better wear   9 had better not ride

10 had better not eat

[Step 1 : 문장 시작하기]   p.55

2 The athlete should practice running.

3 Students should do their homework.

4 Children should not eat caramels.

5 We should not play music.

6 Catherine had better take out the spot.

7 We had better go to the beach.

8 Jason had better wear a coat.

9 Your brother had better not ride a bicycle.

10 You had better not eat food.

[Step 2 : 문장 완성하기]   p.56

2 The famous athlete should practice running.

3 All students should do their homework.

4 Children should not eat many caramels.

5 We should not play loud music.

6 Catherine had better take out the black spot.

7 We had better go to the beautiful beach.

8 Jason had better wear a warm coat.

9 Your little brother had better not ride a bicycle.

10 You had better not eat spicy food.

[Step 3 : 문장 꾸미기]   p.57

2 The famous athlete should practice running for the marathon .

3 All students should do their homework after school .

4 Children should not eat many caramels for their lunch .

5 We should not play loud music at night .

6 Catherine had better take out the black spot with bleach .

7 We had better go to the beautiful beach on vacation .

8 Jason had better wear a warm coat in the cold weather .

9 Your little brother had better not ride a bicycle on the icy road .

10 You had better not eat spicy food before going to bed .

Unit 9 조동사 must, have to

Writing에 필요한 문법 확인]   p.59-60

A. 1 must   2 mustn't   3 mustn't   4 must

B. 1 don't have to   2 has to
   3 doesn't have to   4 will have to

C. 1 will have to write / must write
   2 have to cook   3 must feed
   4 had to meet   5 doesn't have to go

[Warm Up : 표현 만들기]   p.60

2 Jason must wash

3 I have to finish

4 She has to buy

5 They don't have to fix up

6 He doesn't have to do

7 Your mom has to make

8 We have to make money

9 Gary had to send

10 Cindy will have to help

[Step 1 : 문장 시작하기]   p.61

2 Jason must wash his car.

3 I have to finish the project.

4 She has to buy a doll.

5 They don't have to fix up the house.

6 He doesn't have to do his homework.

7 Does your mom have to make a cake?

8 Do we have to make money?

9 Gary had to send the news.

10 Cindy will have to help people.

[Step 2 : 문장 완성하기]   p.62

2 Jason must wash his dirty car.

3 I have to finish the new project.

4 She has to buy a cute doll.

5 They don't have to fix up the old house.

6 He doesn't have to do his math homework.

7 Does your mom have to make a delicious

cake?

8 Do we have to make a lot of money?

9 Gary had to send the urgent news.

10 Cindy will have to help sick people.

[Step 3 : 문장 꾸미기]　　　　　　　p.63

2 Jason must wash his dirty car on Sunday.

3 I have to finish the new project by next month.

4 She has to buy a cute doll for her sister's birthday.

5 They don't have to fix up the old house by next week.

6 He doesn't have to do his math homework on the weekend.

7 Does your mom have to make a delicious cake for the party?

8 Do we have to make a lot of money for a better life?

9 Gary had to send the urgent news to his friend.

10 Cindy will have to help sick people in the hospital.

Check Up 3. Unit 7-9

[More Practice]　　　　　　　　　　p.64

A. 1 We have to make cakes for the school party before the end of April.

　　2 You had better not ride a bicycle in the park during the hot day.

　　3 You cannot use a mobile phone during the performance.

　　4 You can take some flowers from my garden for your mom's birthday gift.

B. 1 You must take this medicine both after breakfast and after dinner to get over your cold.

　　2 This elephant from India can understand some Korean words.

　　3 You should not make a noise at night.

　　4 You should not wash your new sweater in

a washing machine.

[Creative Thinking Activity]　　　　p.65

1 David can swim but he can't repair the car.

2 Justin can sing but he can't cook.

3 Kelly can cook but she can't play the piano.

4 Sophia can play the violin but she can't dance.

5 Brian can play basketball but he can't play the drums.

Unit 10 to부정사 1 (명사 역할)

[Writing에 필요한 문법 확인]　　　　p.67

A. 1 to understand　　2 to travel　　3 To learn

　　4 to carry　　　　　5 to play

B. 1 It is difficult to study math.

　　2 It makes me feel good to swim in this pool.

　　3 It is a lot of fun to visit foreign countries.

　　4 It is necessary to exercise regularly.

　　5 It is exciting to go to a concert.

C. 1 to climb　　2 to eat　　3 to swim　　4 to buy

　　5 to meet

[Warm Up : 표현 만들기]　　　　　　p.68

2 to watch a TV program

3 to have a snowball fight

4 to develop a cure

5 not to take the writing course

6 to eat vegetables

7 to keep the secret

8 to look after the animals

9 to set your goal

10 to master foreign languages

[Step 1 : 문장 시작하기]　　　　　　p.69

2 To watch a TV program is helpful.

= It is helpful to watch a TV program.

3 To have a snowball fight is fun.
  = It is fun to have a snowball fight.

4 He wanted to develop a cure.

5 He decided not to take the writing course.

6 They started to eat vegetables.

7 They promised to keep the secret.

8 His job is to look after the animals.

9 The first step is to set your goal.

10 His New Year's resolution is to master foreign languages.

[Step 2 : 문장 완성하기]   p.70

2 To watch a good TV program is helpful.
  = It is helpful to watch a good TV program.

3 To have a snowball fight with friends is fun.
  = It is fun to have a snowball fight with friends.

4 He wanted to develop a cure for the disease.

5 He decided not to take the three-week writing course.

6 They started to eat raw vegetables.

7 They promised to keep the big secret.

8 His job is to look after the wild animals.

9 The first step is to set your goal clearly.

10 His New Year's resolution is to master five foreign languages.

[Step 3 : 문장 꾸미기]   p.71

2 To watch a good TV program is helpful for children's education.
  = It is helpful for children's education to watch a good TV program.

3 To have a snowball fight with friends after school is fun.
  = It is fun to have a snowball fight with friends after school.

4 He wanted to develop a cure for the disease by the end of the year.

5 He decided not to take the three-week writing course for the summer.

6 They started to eat raw vegetables for better health.

7 They promised to keep the big secret for a lasting friendship.

8 His job is to look after the wild animals in the shelter.

9 The first step is to set your goal clearly for the future.

10 His New Year's resolution is to master five foreign languages for world travel.

Unit 11 to부정사 2 (형용사 역할)

[Writing에 필요한 문법 확인]   p.73

A. 1 명사   2 형용사   3 명사   4 형용사   5 형용사

B. 1 to learn   2 to wear   3 to write with
   4 to do   5 to fix

C. 1 no friends to help   2 person to talk to
   3 books to read   4 paper to write on
   5 a school uniform to wear

[Warm Up : 표현 만들기]   p.74

2 the first Korean to visit

3 friends to play soccer with

4 dishes to wash   5 a house to live in

6 colored pencils to draw with

7 problems to solve   8 boxes to carry

9 something cold to drink

10 money to spend

[Step 1 : 문장 시작하기]   p.75

2 He was the first Korean.

3 I want friends.

4 There were dishes.

5 They owned a house.

6 Mike wants to buy colored pencils.

7 We had problems.

8 Kate had boxes.

9 David wants something cold.

10 The brothers had money.

[Step 2 : 문장 완성하기] p.76

2 He was the first Korean to visit America.

3 I want friends to play soccer with.

4 There were dishes to wash.

5 They owned a house to live in.

6 Mike wants to buy colored pencils to draw with.

7 We had problems to solve.

8 Kate had boxes to carry.

9 David wants something cold to drink.

10 The brothers had money to spend.

[Step 3 : 문장 꾸미기] p.77

2 He was the first Korean to visit America in the Joseon Dynasty.

3 I want friends to play soccer with during a lunch break.

4 There were dishes to wash after the party.

5 They owned a house to live in at the time.

6 Mike wants to buy inexpensive colored pencils to draw with.

7 We had problems to solve during the emergency.

8 Kate had boxes to carry on her moving day.

9 David wants something cold to drink after exercise.

10 The brothers had money to spend on their mom's birthday present.

Unit 12 to부정사 3 (부사 역할)

[Writing에 필요한 문법 확인] p.79-80

A. 1 구입하기 위해서

2 너무 어려서 여행할 수 없는

3 구입할 만큼 충분히 부자인

4 훔칠

5 듣게 되어

B. 1 difficult to make

2 smart enough to join

3 too tired to clean

4 enough money to buy

5 fast enough to catch

C. 1 This chair is not comfortable to sit on.

2 He must be clever to solve the quiz.

3 They were strong enough to win the game.

4 They go to the park after dinner to take a walk.

5 Jen baked a cake to celebrate her mom's birthday.

[Warm Up : 표현 만들기] p.80

2 to catch the bus

3 to see his architecture

4 to maintain health

5 to help poor children

6 to learn Spanish

7 too difficult to master

8 to survive an earthquake

9 enough to move the refrigerator

10 too heavy to cross the bridge

[Step 1 : 문장 시작하기] p.81

2 David ran fast.

3 Jason went to the Gaudi exhibition.

4 Regular exercise is recommended.

5 He will donate some of his savings.

6 Kevin decided to take the class.

7 This language is too difficult.

8 This castle was built.

9 Mike is strong enough.

10 The elephant was too heavy.

[Step 2 : 문장 완성하기] p.82

2 David ran fast to catch the bus.

3 Jason went to the Gaudi exhibition to see his architecture.

4 Regular exercise is recommended to
   maintain health .

5 He will donate some of his savings to help
   poor children .

6 Kevin decided to take the class to learn
   Spanish .

7 This language is too difficult to master .

8 This castle was built to survive an
   earthquake .

9 Mike is strong enough to move the heavy
   refrigerator .

10 The elephant was too heavy to cross the
   wooden bridge .

[Step 3 : 문장 꾸미기]   p.83

2 David ran fast to catch the bus to New York .

3 Jason went to the Gaudi exhibition to see his
   architecture on the weekend .

4 Regular exercise is recommended to maintain
   good health.

5 He will donate some of his savings to help
   poor children in the near future .

6 Kevin decided to take the class to learn
   Spanish after his eight-week visit of Spain .

7 This language is too difficult to master in a
   short time .

8 This castle was built by ancient Egyptians
   to survive an earthquake.

9 Mike is strong enough to move the heavy
   refrigerator twice .

10 The elephant was too heavy to cross the
   wooden bridge in the forest .

Check Up 4. Unit 10-12

[More Practice]   p.84

A. 1 Mike should save money to buy a new car.

   2 Sarah went to the library near her school
     to borrow some books.

   3 It is impossible to solve the math problems
     without a calculator in 30 minutes.

   4 We ran fast to catch the last bus at

night.

B. 1 James went to the supermarket near his
     house to buy some food.

   2 I studied for many hours to get a good
     score on the test.

   3 My plan for this year is to get up early in
     the morning to be on time at school.

   4 You must keep down your voice to follow
     the rules of this library.

[Creative Thinking Activity]   p.85

Mom: Hi Justin and Brian. What do you want to
     do today?

Justin: Sally said the new animation "Cars" is
       good. I want to go to the movie.

Brian: I already saw it with Alice. I want to go
      to a museum or go swimming. What do
      you want to do with us, Mom?

Mom: Going to a museum sounds great, but I
     want to clean the house.

Brian: Oh no, Mom. Today is the hottest day. I
      don't want to do any work.

Justin: Brian is right. I don't want to clean the
       house on this hot day. How about going
       swimming?

Mom: All right, boys. I don't want to go
     swimming, but I am going to go with you.